# BOURNEMOUTH
# PAST

Bournemouth in 1905.

# BOURNEMOUTH PAST

## Elizabeth Edwards

Phillimore

1998

Published by
PHILLIMORE & CO. LTD.,
Shopwyke Manor Barn, Chichester, West Sussex

ISBN 0 85033 962 6

Printed and bound in Great Britain by
BIDDLES LTD.
Guildford, Surrey

# Contents

# List of Illustrations

*Frontispiece*: Bournemouth in 1905

# Acknowledgements

I wish to express acknowledgements and thanks to all those who have encouraged me and expressed interest in my latest book on Bournemouth's history, including: Nigel Beale; H. Insley Fox, H.A. Mellory Pratt, A.H.D. Brownlee of Mooring Aldridge. J.A. Young, Malcolm Fox, Rev. Clifford Curry, Rabbi Sydney Gold, Mrs. R. Cooper, Miss P. Angus, Mrs. Taconis, Mrs. M. Walsh, Roger Guttridge, Elizabeth Collins, Barbara Warde, W. Letts, Betty Summerell, Graham Teasdill, Robert Baggs, Kathleen Lawrence and Jim Boudreau.

I wish to thank the following for the loan or gift of many photographs: Mrs. K. Spackman of Bournemouth Reference Library and by courtesy of Bournemouth's Local Studies Collection, the Public Relations and Publicity Dept. of Bournemouth Borough Unitary Council, Mr. Peter Hayward, Mace Bearer, Rowan White Photographic, Ted Hughes (former fireman), Max Bygraves, Irene Richmond, Edna Dawes, Harry L. Edwards, Jack Inglis, Bill Maguire, Russell-Cotes Art Gallery & Museum, Desmond Tarrant, Vernon Preston, Colin Caddy and Jim Boudreau Collection, Jan Fostekew, Simon Dursley, Business Planner, Royal Bournemouth Hospital, Fabian Society, Alan Ivamy, Herbert Hospital, Wentworth College, Miss Austin Smith, Mrs. M. Walsh, Mr. Kiddle.

Line Drawings: Harry L. Edwards.

The Local Studies booklets were a source of help to me as they were when I wrote *A History of Bournemouth* (1981). If I have inadvertently omitted to acknowledge anyone, I do give my sincerest apologies.

*In Memory of My Husband*

## CHAPTER ONE

# Early Days

## Hengistbury Head

Some people still consider Bournemouth a new town although beneath its soil are many valuable traces of antiquity.

One of the most important archaeological sites in the country is Hengistbury Head and its stark jutting out headland, Warren Hill. The first occupation of Hengistbury seems to have been during the latter part of the old Stone Age, *c.*9000 B.C., when primitive groups of hunters arrived to slay and eat reindeer and other animals.

Later Stone-Age men preferred to live near the coast on the banks of the rivers when farming skills were developed. From about 1900 B.C. to 600 B.C. was the Bronze Age when men discovered how to make metal tools. Their important personages were buried in round barrows or tumuli, after cremation and with many of their possessions besides them. Long barrows and burial urns have been discovered at Moordown, Iford, Longbarrow Road and a complete cemetery at Hillbrow, Pokesdown. In the Iron Age Hengistbury became one of

**1**  Hengistbury Head Memorial to Charles E. Smith who was accidentally shot whilst he was shooting rabbits on Hengistbury Head. Due to cliff erosion the monument was twice moved and is now in the churchyard of St James the Greater, Pokesdown.

2 Alum Chine, where mining work was carried out by the 6th Baron Mountjoy—and also in other areas.

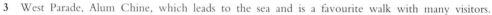

3 West Parade, Alum Chine, which leads to the sea and is a favourite walk with many visitors.

the busiest trading posts in Southern Britain. For defence they built banks and ditches and the famous Double Dykes.

In the 16th century James Blount, 6th Baron Mountjoy, Lord of Canford Manor, formed a trading venture in the area. He discovered that alum lay beneath the soil at Parkstone. He began to produce copperas and to boil alum which was then used in tanning and other trades. The venture was unsuccessful; the only reminder of it is the name 'Alum Chine' given to a well-wooded, narrow ravine in one of the mining areas and a favourite walk with many visitors.

## Holdenhurst,
## the Mother of Bournemouth

The development of Bournemouth as a fashionable seaside resort only commenced in the 19th century. As it expanded it absorbed several old communities whose forefathers had lived on the banks of the river Stour and tilled the soil for many generations. Thomas Hardy described Bournemouth as a 'pleasure city and glittering novelty' which had sprung up on 'a tawny piece of antiquity ... a new world in an old one'.

The old world comprised parts of the parish of Christchurch and mainly of the ancient village and chapelry of Holdenhurst, sometimes referred to as the 'forgotten village'. It was from this rural area that Bournemouth, then wild heathland, slowly grew.

The village first appears in the Domesday Survey of 1086. This is the translation:

The King himself holds HOLEEST [HOLDENHURST] ... Land for 20 ploughs ... 37 villagers and 25 smallholders with 19 ploughs.

A small church; 14 slaves; a mill at 15s.; 3 fisheries ...

The word 'Holeest' is derived from the Old English 'holegn' or 'holly' and 'hyrst' and became Holdenhurst in the 18th century.

The focus of village life was the church. By 1829 the Saxon building was in need of repair and only seated 200 parishioners, the population then being about six hundred and twenty. Land near the old church was given by Sir George Ivison Tapps, Lord of the Manor of Christchurch, and by 1834 a new church, dedicated to St John the Evangelist, was built to seat 472 people. Until 1829, when Sir George gave land for the purpose, there was no burial ground in Holdenhurst. Previously

**4**   The Church of St John the Evangelist, Holdenhurst, drawn by Harry L. Edwards. The church was built in 1834 and replaced an old Saxon one. Members of the Cooper-Dean family are buried in the churchyard.

**5** Part of the village green of Holdenhurst showing Magdalen Cottage (the old cottage) and part of the Lepers' Hospital in its back garden.

**6** Lepers' Hospital, about 500 years old and showing the emaciated head and rib cage of a leper.

part of the graveyard of Christchurch Priory had been set apart for the burial of Holdenhurst's deceased, for which the church-warden paid a rent of 2s. annually to the priory. Facing the centuries-old village green are the New House and the Old House or Magdalen Cottage; the latter, with its thatched roof and beams, is probably 17th-century. Standing in its garden is a low, half-timbered building, about five hundred years old, often referred to as the Lepers Hospital. On its walls are the carvings of the emaciated head and rib cage of a leper.

Opposite the vicarage was the village school, built by subscription *c.*1846 (closed in 1948) mainly by the then Earl of Malmesbury of Hurn Court, who also provided the land, and by Mr. Clapcott-Dean (a member of the Cooper-Dean family), the two principal land-owners in Holdenhurst village. Hurn Court was the home of the Malmesbury family from 1800 to 1950 when it became a boarding school for boys. Originally it was the country house and manor farm of the Priors of Christchurch.

Other adjoining Saxon villages are Throop, Muccleshell and Muscliff and also Throop Mill.

**7** Ellen Cooper-Dean, the last member of the Cooper-Dean family, who died in November 1984. The family were landowners and great benefactors to Bournemouth.

**8** Littledown House, home of the Cooper-Deans of Holdenhurst, built *c*.1789.

**9** The Old Saxon Mill, Throop, mentioned in the Domesday Survey as worth 15s. Milling was carried on there until 1974.

**10** Cis Biles, the last miller, who worked there for 52 years, loving every minute of it. His last wish was to die in the mill, which is what actually happened.

## Before Bournemouth

In the 18th century there was no such place as Bournemouth, although the words 'La Bournemowthe' are shown in the Christchurch cartulary of 1407; but this was a geographical reference to the little Bourne (burna) stream which was to give Bournemouth its name. In a Calendar of Domestic State Papers of 1574, Lord Thomas Poulet, Earl of Southampton, reported:

> We finde at Bourne Mouthe within the west bay at Christchurche a place very easy for the enemye to lande being voyde of all inhabiting. (Public Record Office)

From an area of wild barren heathland, steep, rocky cliffs descending to golden, uninhabited sands, narrow chines and dense woods, to a fashionable, popular holiday resort in 190 years is quite remarkable. But more remarkable is that this fine, elegant town owes its beginning to smuggling which was rife in the late 18th and early 19th centuries. This desolate area with its empty, golden sands proved an ideal place for the illicit trade of smuggling.

The 18th and 19th centuries were periods of poverty, unemployment and high taxes, mainly caused by the wars against France. There were blockades of foreign goods, and the taxes exacted by excise men made the prices prohibitive to many people. It was said that during the reign of George III more goods were smuggled into the country than came in legitimately.

## Smuggler Gulliver and his Followers

Villagers living nearby in small, scattered communities were mainly farm workers or fishermen, often earning less than ten shillings a week. It is not surprising that most of them aided the smugglers when, although the risks were great, so too were the rewards—usually ten shillings for one night's work. The chief smuggler was Isaac Gulliver (1745-1822),

**11** Isaac Gulliver and his followers. The photo was taken by Robert Day, the first photographer in Bournemouth, from a painting by Henry Perlee Parker. The painting used to be in the *Tregonwell Arms*.

To the Memory of
ROBERT TROTMAN
*Late of Rond in the County
of Wilts* who was barbaroufly
Murder'd on the Shore near
*Poole* the 24 March 1765

A little Tea one leaf I did not fteal
For Guiltlefs Blood shed I to GOD appeal
Put Tea in one scale human Blood in tother
And think what tis to flay thy harmlefs Brother

**12** Robert Trotman's grave. He was killed in a clash between the revenue officers and smugglers. Sympathies were for the smugglers.

who employed as many as 50 men. His fast sailing craft moved swiftly and surreptitiously, carrying contraband from the continent into rocky coves on the deserted sands of the Bourne area, where they were met by 'landers' with pack horses, who hid the goods until they could be disposed of safely. Even the gentry assisted and were pleased to receive barrels of brandy and rum, and laces and silks for their ladies.

An Act of 1736 imposed the death penalty for wounding an excise officer and five years' transportation for resisting arrest, but few were deterred. The feelings of the local people were shown by the inscription on a smuggler's grave at St Andrew's Church, Kinson (Kingston):

> To the Memory of ROBERT TROTMAN Late of Rond in the County of Wilts who was barbarously Murdered on the Shore near Poole the 24 March 1765.

**13** St Andrew's Church, Kinson, known as 'The Smugglers' Church', is of Saxon origin, although only the tower foundation remains.

**14** The *Tregonwell Arms* in 1883. It was a favourite haunt of smugglers and became the first Post Office, when in 1839 Mr. Fox became 'Receiver' and when letters were often sorted on the counter.

St Andrew's Church was often known as 'the Smugglers' church. Casks and bales of smuggled goods were hidden in its belfry, while grooves in its stone parapets were made by the constant friction of ropes hauling kegs of brandy and other merchandise to the tower.

Isaac Gulliver earned fame and wealth through his illegal activities. In 1782 a free pardon was granted to smugglers who would serve in the Navy or provide a substitute. Gulliver provided a substitute, although, when he discovered a plot against the life of King George III, the king was supposed to have said, 'Let Gulliver smuggle as much as he likes'.

Gulliver retired to Gulliver's House at Wimborne, entered into partnership with a banker and even became a churchwarden. He was buried in the centre aisle, under the clock tower, at Wimborne Minster.

To defeat the smugglers, the government appointed excise officers who were stationed at Christchurch. Also stationed with the Dorset Rangers at the newly built Barracks there was Captain Lewis Tregonwell and his lieutenant son, St. Barbe Tregonwell. Their duties were to guard the coastline, to warn of any attempted invasion and to help the excise men in the prevention of smuggling. Lewis Tregonwell was to become the Founder of Bournemouth.

**15**  Lewis Dymoke Grosvenor Tregonwell, the Founder of Bournemouth (1758-1832). He was captain of the Dorset Yeomanry and his duty was to prevent the enemy from landing during the Napoleonic wars and to help the Customs and Excise men in preventing smuggling.

## The Founder of Bournemouth

The name 'Tregonwell' comes from an ancient seat in Cornwall, prior to the Norman period. It is stated in Hutchins' *History and Antiquities*, 'Tregonwell of Bellarmine builded many places and had many lands and manors ...'.

Lewis Dymoke Grosvenor Tregonwell (1758-1832), J.P., Squire of Cranborne Lodge, was the son of Thomas Tregonwell, of Anderson, Dorset. From the 17th century two branches of the family developed, the Tregonwells of Milton Abbey and the Tregonwells of Winterborne Anderson. It was to the latter branch that Lewis Tregonwell belonged.

After retiring from the army in 1810 Lewis Tregonwell and his second wife, Henrietta, daughter of H.W. Portman of Orchard Portman and Bryanston, Dorset, spent some time in Muddiford (Mudeford), a select sea-bathing area which had become popular through visits from King George III. Henrietta was unhappy and suffering in health from the unexpected death of her baby son, Grosvenor, on the day he should have been baptised. On 14 July 1810 Lewis decided to give his wife a pleasant outing to the area of the Bourne that he had previously patrolled. Bourne still consisted of wild, swampy heathland and dense forests, but Lewis also remembered the beauty of the coastline and the golden sands.

Henrietta was charmed with the beauty of the bay, the wild gorse growing in profusion and the pine forests with their aroma which was later to attract wealthy invalids to Bourne. She suggested that it would be ideal to have a holiday residence in this delightful area. Lewis, anxious to please her, readily agreed. His first step was to purchase 8½ acres of land near the sea from Sir George Ivison Tapps, Lord of the Manor of Christchurch, for £179 11s. 0d. Here the first house in Bourne (later Bournemouth) was built, known originally as The Mansion. In 1814 Lewis Tregonwell bought further land from Sir George at £40 an acre and in 1822 land at £60 an acre.

His estate became known as Bourne Tregonwell and extended from the sea to Yelverton Road, off Old Christchurch Road. He then acquired the *Tapps Arms*, built in 1809 in nearby Beckford Road (today Post Office Road), the only public house after the *New Inn* in Iford and a favourite haunt of smugglers. It was also used as the first Post Office. The inn was practically rebuilt and renamed the *Tregonwell Arms*; it was demolished in 1885 to the sorrow of those who admired the picturesque inn.

**16**  The Mansion, the first house in Bourne. Lewis Tregonwell was the Squire of Cranborne and the Mansion was regarded as the Tregonwells' holiday home where they spent enjoyable periods by the sea and beach.

The Mansion was first occupied by the Tregonwells on 24 April 1812 and became their summer residence. A cottage was erected for their butler, Symes, first known as Symes Cottage and later as Portman Lodge, after Mrs. Tregonwell's maiden name; there she lived and died after the death of her husband. After being destroyed by fire, an underground chamber, with a trap door, was discovered. It has been suggested that Symes might have been in league with the smugglers!

In the early days friends were invited to visit The Mansion, and soon extra cottages were built for letting—the beginning of seaside

**17** Exeter House after extensions. Friends were invited and afterwards lettings commenced to select visitors.

TO THE MEMORY OF
**LEWIS D. G. TREGONWELL**
WHO ERECTED THE FIRST HOUSE
IN BOURNEMOUTH ON THIS SITE IN 1810.
HE DIED ON JAN. 18TH 1832. AGED 73.
AND WAS BURIED IN
ST. PETER'S CHURCHYARD. BOURNEMOUTH.
HE WAS DESCENDED FROM SIR JOHN TREGONWELL
A MEMBER OF AN ANCIENT CORNISH FAMILY.

THIS TABLET IS ERECTED BY MEMBERS OF THE
BOURNEMOUTH AND DISTRICT CORNISH
ASSOCIATION AND FRIENDS. OCT. 1937.

**18** The Tregonwell plaque outside the *Exeter Hotel*.

holidays. An advertisement appeared in a newspaper that The Mansion was to let furnished:

> A modern, detached house at Bourne Mouth, between Poole and Christchurch with three parlours, six or seven bedrooms, kitchen, scullery, stable for two horses and a bathing machine ... Cows are kept on the spot.

After the Marchioness of Exeter with all her retinue became the first tenant, the Mansion became Exeter House and the road was renamed Exeter Road to commemorate her visit. In 1876 the house was purchased by Henry Newlyn, who extended the Mansion, and it became known as *Newlyn's Family Hotel*. After members of the royal family had stayed there it acquired its present name, the *Royal Exeter Hotel*.

Lewis Tregonwell died in 1832 and was first buried at Winterbourne Anderson. After the consecration of St Peter's Church, the first parish church in Bournemouth, his remains were transferred there on 26 February 1846, and also those of his son, Grosvenor. After her husband's death Mrs. Tregonwell sold part of their land and received £800 per acre! She died in 1846 at Portman Lodge where she was then living.

CHAPTER TWO

# A Health Resort

## The Development of Bourne

Though Lewis Tregonwell was the founder of Bournemouth, much of its growth was due to the foresight and enterprise of the Tapps-Gervis-Meyrick family. Sir George Ivison Tapps (ancestor of the present Sir George Meyrick), became lord of the manor of Christchurch and liberty of Westover, in which Bourne was situated. On his death in March 1835 he was suceeded by his son, Sir George William Tapps Gervis, M.P. for Christchurch, who continued the work commenced by his father. He not only envisaged a marine village, a growing seaside resort for the genteel elderly and those in delicate health, but in which a church *must* be included.

19   Westover Shrubbery showing the area overgrown with trees and bushes.

20   Westover Villas in 1840. The first 16 villas were built on the instructions of Sir George Ivison Tapps, Lord of the Manor, who envisaged Bourne as a select letting area.

With this in mind he commissioned a young architect, Benjamin Ferrey, a pupil of Augustus Pugin, to design a future health resort. Ferrey's suggestions resulted in the building of 16 Westover Villas in 1837, the first villas to be erected in Bourne. Sir George stipulated that every villa should be detached, in its own grounds, and Tudor, Gothic or Italian in style.

The same year Ferry designed an elegant hotel, the *Bath Hotel*, which was opened with ceremony by Sir George Gervis on the coronation day of Queen Victoria on 28 June 1838. The tariff was four guineas a week for a month's holiday! It became known as *Royal Bath Hotel* after members of royalty had stayed there, including Prince Oscar of Sweden, Empress Eugénie (widow of Napoleon III), King Edward VII as a young boy and others. A more modest building, Belle Vue Boarding House (later hotel), was also erected 'for those who preferred a quiet and retired mode of life'

(*Visitors' Guide Book* of 1840); it was replaced in 1929 by the fine Pavilion and Assembly Rooms of today.

Ferrey's plans also included a number of villas in different styles to be erected on the cliff front. In *Tess of the D'Urbervilles* Thomas Hardy wrote admiringly of 'the lofty roofs, chimneys, gazebos and towers of the numerous fanciful residences of which the place was composed' and describes the place as 'a city of detached mansions; a Mediterranean lounging place on the English Channel'.

Ferrey's plans for a church, based on an eight-sided building with lancet windows and an ornamental turret and spire on a site further up the hill than the present St Peter's Church, were not accepted. Visitors still had to travel to Poole, Christchurch and Holdenhurst (in whose parish and chapelry the land which became Bournemouth was situated) for church services.

**21** *Bath Hotel* in 1845, the first purpose-built hotel in Bourne. It was opened with ceremony on 28 June 1838, the coronation day of Queen Victoria.

22 *Bath Hotel* in 1865—there are still plenty of open spaces outside the hotel.

23 *Royal Bath Hotel*, 1890. The hotel was purchased by Merton Russell Cotes in 1876. It was considerably extended to become a place where he was able to display his wonderful collections from abroad.

The Belle Vue Hotel Library and Baths
BOURNEMOUTH.

**24**  The *Belle Vue Hotel* was said to cater for those who preferred a retired and quiet mode of life. It was demolished in 1929 to be replaced by the present Pavilion.

It was a great disappointment to the chief landowners and developers when, on reading the book *Spas of England* written in 1840 by Dr. A. Granville, a well-known London physician, that there was no mention whatever of Bourne. Fortunately, the following year he was again in the vicinity of 'the unknown terrain' and received a pressing invitation.

This time he extolled the virtues of the undiscovered haven 'of which he was entirely unaware when he wrote his first book'. His report was ecstatic: 'I look upon Bourne as a perfect discovery among the sea nooks one longs to have for a real invalid'. In his opinion there was no place along the south coast that possessed so much potential, including excellent sea bathing, for being the first invalid sea-watering place in England, particularly as a winter residence for the most delicate constitutions. To conclude, he stressed the importance of a church, but condemned the position chosen by Ferrey: 'Visitors would be blown away before they had reached the top of the hill'. Pines had been planted in about 1802 by the lord of the manor and other land-owners. The aroma and perfume of these trees were considered health-giving, so that more doctors recommended Bourne to their wealthy and often consumptive patients. Bourne became known as a 'bath chair town'.

## Mont Dore Hotel

Dr. Dobell was a London physician who came to live in Bournemouth from 1882 although previously he had stayed there, finding relaxation from his London practice. He had also visited the Auvergne in France where he had been most impressed by the Mont Dore cure given at the famous spa of that name. In his book *Medical Aspects of Bournemouth and its Surroundings* he wrote,

> I consider the heathland character of the site of Bournemouth of utmost importance in its medical aspects and much gratitude is due to the early planners for not building houses under the cliffs but on them.

To some of the chief medical men in Bournemouth he wrote,

> I propose to establish at Bournemouth a system of treatment similar to that in the Auvergne, known as the Mont Dore cure and consider that the treatment might be more successfully carried out in Bournemouth than at Mont Dore.

Dr. Dobell considered that the balm and resinous perfume from the pines would be most beneficial to those with consumptive and bronchial complaints. The Mont Dore cure when introduced, would relieve many other types of disorders, including rheumatism, gout, scrofula and syphilis.

**25** The *Mont Dore Hotel*, 1885, a luxurious hotel which provided the Mont Dore cure and in 1921 became the present Town Hall.

In May 1881 the foundation stone was laid by King Oscar II of Sweden and Norway who had been staying at the *Crag Head* in Manor Road (today a high rise block of flats) with Queen Sophie Wilhelmina, who had been ill for many years, but the health-giving charms of Bournemouth had effected a cure. The king was only too happy to extol the many curative virtues of the area.

The *Mont Dore Hotel* was opened in 1885 with every conceivable luxury. It was the first residential hotel to be built so far back from the seafront. It was constructed in an Italian style of architecture on four acres of land

previously known as 'The Glen', and was described as the most magnificent in the south of England. There were superbly decorated sitting rooms, drawing rooms, billiard and smoking rooms, a covered tennis court, outdoor skating and a ballroom. It even possessed a telephone, one of the first in England and the number was 3.

Above everything the hotel offered the Mont Dore cure. The water vital to the health of the many patients who flocked to this palatial establishment was imported from the springs of the Auvergne. This water contained essential constituents which could not be found

**26** Bournemouth's present Town Hall, 1921, and War Memorial, 1922-3, as seen from the Upper Gardens. The first Town Hall was erected in Town Hall Avenue (now the Criterion Arcade), and the second in Yelverton Road in 1892.

anywhere else in England including carbonic acid gas, nitrogen, helium and mineral contents of iron. The water could be gargled and its vapours inhaled. Sea and pure water from the Bourne were pumped into the basement of the hotel to allow the additional luxury of soaking and perspiring in Turkish and salt baths. The hotel was also open to non-residents.

To ensure that the correct treatments were given Dr. Dobell arranged for Dr. Edmond, chief physician at Mont Dore, Auvergne, to reside in the *Mont Dore Hotel*, Bournemouth and supervise the treatment during the bitterly cold winter months when the French establishment was closed. Bournemouth's reputation was firmly established as a select watering place for the wealthy and the delicate.

When the First World War commenced in 1914 the hotel was commandeered by the army for a hospital. First there were Indian soldiers, then British soldiers, and finally it was a convalescent home for officers until May 1919 when it was sold. It became Bournemouth's present Town Hall in 1921. (Previous Town Halls were in Town Hall Square [now Criterion Arcade] and the second one was in Yelverton Road.)

## CHAPTER THREE

# Church and Religion

## We Must Have A Church

There had to be a church of some kind. Two semi-detached cottages, erected in 1838 (near the present Debenham's stores), were knocked into one. It was used as a church on Sundays and a schoolroom during the week, but the small building accommodated less than two-thirds of the population. As more seaside villas were built and more people were attracted to the new watering place, the need for a church became even more imperative.

Sir George appointed a new architect in 1841, John Tulloch of Poole and Wimborne. On 28 September a foundation stone was laid, which read: 'This church was built at the sole expense of Sir William Tapps-Gervis, Bart, of Hinton Admiral in the county of Hants. and proprietor of this estate.' When it was completed, its plain, ugly, mock Gothic style was criticised for being 'all height and no length'. There were no decorations and the interior was plain and austere. It seated

**27**  The first St Peter's Church, c.1842, disliked by most as ugly and plain.

**28** St Peter's Church with tower and No. 1, Westover Villas.

150 persons and 90 in the gallery. In 1851 the population of Bourne was 695 which by 1861 increased to 1,707, the church was too small!

For two years the church remained empty as no clergyman could be persuaded to accept the unattractive living. There was no parsonage, no church school and a small endowment of £50 a year. In 1845, to the relief of many residents, the Rev. Alexander Morden Bennett was inducted as the first vicar. He remarked that when he came to Bourne the church was a very poor structure. Another architect was appointed to design a new church, George E. Street, diocesan clerk of Oxford. Morden Bennett realised that it was important to have

a fine church to match the promise of the growing town. Owing to the expense and difficulties, the work was carried out over a period of 30 years and in three stages. It started with a new north aisle and 12 lancet windows. A tower was added and finally, a spire which, with its cross, stood 202 feet above the ground.

For 26 years Morden Bennett and his architect worked happily together. Sadly, on 19 January 1880, only one month after completion the Rev. Morden Bennett died. Over 3,000 people attended his funeral to show their love and respect for their first vicar. He was buried to the right of the 39 steps to recall the 39 Articles. George Street died the following year.

**29** The spire and cross were added. The improved St Peter's materialised after alterations had lasted for about 30 years.

**30** St Peter's School, the first purpose-built National School, was opened in 1850 on land adjoining the church. It was demolished *c*.1936.

**31** General view of Bournemouth, 1905. St Andrew's Presbyterian Church (now U.R.) in Exeter Road, is on the left. Richmond Hill Congregational (now U.R.) is on the right.

Many renowned people have been connected with St Peter's Church. John Keble, vicar of Hursley in the New Forest, Professor of Poetry at Oxford University and pioneer of the Oxford Movement came to Bournemouth in 1865 with his wife, hoping that the healing qualities of the watering place would improve her poor health. They stayed in a boarding house, Brookside in Exeter Lane, now *Hermitage Hotel*, where he died in March 1866. The original Italianate-style tower still remains. In memory of this devout preacher two stained-glass windows were erected near his favourite place, showing him wearing his cassock, surplice and hood. In 1906 the south transept was made into a side-chapel, named in his memory.

In 1898 the former Liberal Prime Minister, William Ewart Gladstone, took his last communion at St Peter's shortly before his death. A brass plate on the end stall commemorates the event on Thursday, 3 March 1898. He died shortly afterwards at his home in Hawarden.

Other famous graves include those of the Tregonwell family, the Shelley family, Sir Dan Godfrey, and Constantin Silvestri, the conductor.

## A Period of Religious Growth

Religion played a great part in the lives of the Victorians; it is not surprising, therefore, that as the marine village expanded there was an accompanying growth in church building. Most people were High Church and small churches soon had to be made into larger ones.

The development of St Peter's, the first church in the marine village, from two cottages to the elegant building and landmark of today, reflects the growth of the district.

Other religions were attracted to the sea-side area. Congregationalism developed from groups of Protestant dissenters, resulting from pioneer work from ministers and members of Poole and Christchurch churches which had existed since the 17th century.

Pokesdown Congregation (now United Reformed) Church, founded in 1820 in a

**32**   Dr. J.D. Jones, a sincere and popular minister at Richmond Hill Congregational Church. Through his work and that of other Free Church members, the Collegiate School for girls was founded in 1899 to provide a sound Christian education. (Now Wentworth College.)

thatched cottage, was the only Free Church between Poole and Christchurch. It was started by Dr. Daniel Gunn, a fervent preacher from Christchurch. Services were started in Bournemouth in 1848 in a house in Poole Road, then in a small chapel in Orchard Street the following year. When a larger church became necessary, its present site on one of the most commanding positions in the town was donated by G. Durrant. On 4 July 1854 a foundation stone was laid by G.O. Aldridge, who became the first deacon of Richmond Hill Congregation Church. After five years of problems the church was completed in 1859. By 1891 a larger church was required which opened on the same site as its predecessor.

In 1898 Dr. J.D. Jones was appointed whose sincerity and compelling manner attracted visitors from far and wide to listen to 'Jones of Bournemouth'. Due to his vision and enterprise as an educationalist and author, the Bournemouth Collegiate School was founded— now Wentworth College (see Chapter Six).

**33**   Wentworth Milton Mount School (now Wentworth College). The original part of the school was the home of Lord Portman until 1922 when it was purchased by Dr. Jones. For many years it has been a successful independent day and boarding school for girls.

After 39 years of managing a large church he retired. Moving tributes were made and Dr. Jones was made a Companion of Honour and presented with the Freedom of the Borough.

Many well known Bournemouth names have been associated with the development of the church including Beales, Mooring Aldridge's, Bright's, Hankinson and many mayors and other residents.

Another early church is St Andrew's Presbyterian (now United Reformed) Church, originally referred to as the 'Scotch Church'. An unattractive building of galvanised iron was erected in 1857 at the foot of Richmond Hill by the Rev. McMillan, who, like many others, had come to Bournemouth for his health. In 1872 the iron building was demolished and the foundation stone for a new church was laid that year. When the Rev. Rodgers of Wolverhampton became the pastor in 1885, due to his sincere and able preaching the church became overcrowded again and in 1886 land was acquired in Exeter Road where the third and present church stands.

Methodism started in Bournemouth due to the initiative of Poole members, who in 1859 rented simple quarters in Orchard Street, followed by a temporary building purchased in 1866. Other temporary buildings were used until, by 1883 needing a larger building, a new, Gothic-style church was erected on Richmond Hill in 1886. The church was named the Punshon Memorial Church in memory of Dr. W. Morley Punshon, a highly esteemed preacher of wisdom and vision. In 1943 the church was demolished by an enemy bomb just one hour after morning worship. After using temporary buildings again a new site was obtained in Exeter Road. In December 1958 the new church was dedicated by the Rev. Leslie Weatherhead, the former president of the Methodist Conference. The architect, Ronald Sims, was awarded a bronze medal from the Royal Institute of British Architects for his elegant, modern church with its outstanding tower of brick and glass rising 60 ft. above the ground, continuing to a slender spire and surmounted by an alloy cross 132 ft. above the ground. The church is also noted for the special interest it takes in holiday makers.

When it was realised by the Rev. Morden Bennett that a church and school on the west side of the town was required, land was secured in St Michael's Road. George Street, the main architect of St Peter's Church, was commissioned to build the new church, called St Michael's and All Angels'. Morden Bennett, although pleased with the barn-like church, began to work for a larger and more permanent building. Norman Shaw, a pupil of Street's, became the architect, and the foundation stone was laid by Morden Bennett in 1874. After the first part of the church was completed in Early English style, the 'old barn' was demolished to the regret of many residents.

**34** The modern Punshon Memorial Church in Exeter Road built in memory of Dr. Morley Punshon, 1958. The previous church was demolished by a bomb in 1943.

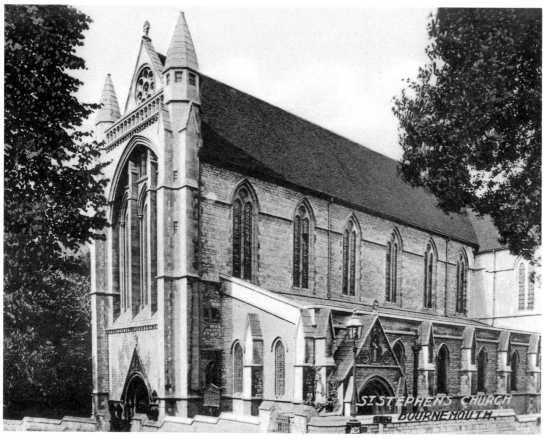

**35** St Stephen's Church was erected in memory of Rev. A. Morden Bennett who died in 1880. The beautiful church is said to be like a cathedral in miniature.

St Stephen's Church is often referred to as the Bennett Memorial Church as it was built to commemorate the memory of the Rev. Morden Bennett, who died in 1880. Like most churches in Bournemouth, the church started in a temporary building in 1881 and a memorial stone for the permanent church was laid on the same date, as it was the anniversary of Morden Bennett's birth. The church was designed by John Loughborough Pearson, the architect responsible for Truro Cathedral, and in character the church is very like a cathedral. The Rev. A.S. Bennett, the son of Morden Bennett, was the first vicar and maintained the Oxford or Tractarian services.

On 15 March 1888 Prince Oscar, the second son of King Oscar II of Norway and Sweden, married Ebba Munck of Fulkila, at St Stephen's Church, Bournemouth, when he assumed the title of Prince Bernadotte and renounced his claim to the Swedish throne.

By 1874 a few Baptists resided in Bournemouth and felt that their denomination should be represented in the town. As their members were scattered over a wide area, it was decided to build a chapel in Boscombe and another one at Lansdowne. When contributions reached £1,200 a foundation stone was laid in Boscombe on 1 October 1874 and a second foundation stone was laid in Lansdowne by Sir Morton Peto in 1875. Several extensions have taken place to accommodate the growing congregation and to make space for the many visitors who attend both services.

When several sisters of the Congregation of the Cross from St Quintin, Northern France, came to England, the Jesuit Fathers of the Society of Jesus encouraged them to make a foundation in Bournemouth. They stayed at Astney Lodge, St Stephen's Road, where meetings of Catholic ladies were held. In 1871 they moved to 'Mineham' which became the Convent of St Joseph and a convalescent home. In 1886 they moved to Boscombe and purchased land near the sea. A small iron chapel was erected there which was called the Church of the Holy Cross, until the new church of Corpus Christi was constructed and opened in 1896 by Bishop Vertue. The beautiful church was designed in Early-English style with mellow, red bricks and stone dressings. The church, with its increasing congregation, was enlarged c.1933, when a magnificent tower 108 ft. high was surmounted by an 8 ft. high iron cross.

In September 1888 a new convent was blessed—an immense, solid building in Tudor style, each final gable surmounted by a stone cross. The large building, the dearth of religious vocations and changes in the educational system, caused the convent and school to close in 1980, many of the pupils being transferred to St Peter's School in Southbourne. (The convent was sold to the International College of Chiropractors.)

Until 1861 the nearest Catholic church to Bournemouth was at Poole. In 1869 the first public chapel and presbytery was opened by Fathers Brownhill and Eccles at Astney Lodge, St Stephens Road, later replaced by a wooden chapel to accommodate the growing number of worshippers. In February 1875 the first Oratory of the Sacred Heart was consecrated by Dr. Dannell, the Bishop of Southwark. When an extension was again required, which was opened in 1900, an early

**36**   The Convent of the Cross. The nuns had become fewer in number for such a large convent which was sold to the College of Chiropractors.

French-Gothic style was adopted in both the old and new parts.

It was not until about 1900 that Bournemouth had any Jewish residents, when for the next six years services were held in the Belle Vue Assembly Rooms. As the congregation increased it became necessary to have their own synagogue. Land in Wootton Gardens was obtained at a small ground rent from Sir George Meyrick and in 1910 a foundation stone was laid by Albert Samuel, brother of Herbert Samuel, a former High Commissioner for Palestine. The building accommodated 140 gentlemen downstairs and 120 ladies upstairs, in accordance with Hebrew custom. As more Jewish people were attracted to Bournemouth a larger synagogue was required which was re-

consecrated in 1962. The main feature of the original synagogue, the ark, had stained glass windows bearing the ten commandments and this part was retained.

In 1954 a new Reform Synagogue was opened in Christchurch Road. Through welfare organisations and Jewish care funds a blind and convalescent home has been opened while a Home for Aged Jews offers orthodox facilities.

The Society of Friends was formed in 1652 by George Fox. There was no Bournemouth Meeting House until 1871 when one was opened in Avenue Road in the centre of the growing town. A larger building was erected in 1911 on the same site at a cost of £1,313. In 1964 they were approached by Marks & Spencer who wished to extend their

**37**  The Quaker Meeting House in Boscombe. It was a gift from Marks & Spencer in return for the Quakers' old building in Avenue Road.

**38** One of the 75 panels from the Quaker Tapestry, worked by Quakers throughout the world. It has been exhibited in Bournemouth and many other places.

store through to Avenue Road. If the Friends (Quakers) would allow them to have their site, they would erect a new Meeting House wherever they liked in Bournemouth at no cost whatever and with plenty of parking space.

As their Meeting House had again become too small and parking had been prohibited in Avenue Road, they were more than delighted. They chose a site in Wharncliffe Road, Boscombe, where the present fine building was erected in spacious grounds, with a large car park and a special flat for the warden. One of the workmen, originally trained by a Quaker carpenter, later

admitted that he felt the hand of his master instructing and encouraging him to do his very best work. Quakerism is unique as there is no preacher and no creed. Members sit in silent contemplation, listening for the word of God within, when some might feel moved to speak of their spiritual experience.

A Quaker tapestry was commenced in 1981 showing 300 years of Quakerism from its early days with pioneers George Fox and Elizabeth Fry, their hardships and persecution, and a faith which is still as strong today. The beautiful tapestry was worked by Quakers of all ages throughout the world and has been exhibited and admired in many countries.

Emanuel Swedenborg, 1688-1772, was born in Sweden. When he was 55, through study of theology, science, anatomy and a detailed study of the Bible, he felt that his sight had been opened to a new spiritual world. After his death the first New Church was opened in London and in 1950 the first New Church was erected in Bournemouth. Two halls were built in the village of Tuckton for fellowship and worship. In 1958 the present-day modern church was added. With an extension and a church field many activities are provided. Swedenborg said 'True worship consists of being useful, in giving loving service, attending a place of worship for teaching and prayer ...'. The many activities of the New Church play an important part in the life of the community, widening their knowledge, and like Swedenborg, bringing them closer to God, and often revealing latent talents.

Allied to the church is Project Dove, a residential care home, which caters for a wide range of people from the independent, the lonely, those who are completely dependent on the care of others and the mentally handicapped. They all receive love and care in the delightful house which used to be the manse.

The Salvation Army was founded in London, to help the poor and destitute, by William Booth, a Methodist Minister, in 1865. In Bournemouth, it started in the early 1880s with the combination of Pokesdown and Boscombe. Due to the smallness of the Pokesdown building in Woodside Road and an increasing congregation, the corps split.

Boscombe started its own corps in 1885 in Shelley Road and later moved to its own building in Palmerston Road in 1898, and became known as the Boscombe Citadel. When the Boscombe church became old and dilapidated a new modern one was constructed called The Orsborn Memorial Hall in memory of General and Mrs. A. Orsborn, who retired from Australia to Bournemouth in 1934, the first Salvation Army leaders to reside in Britain after retirement. He died in 1967 and the spacious

Memorial Halls were opened in November 1984 to honour the greatly respected General and his wife.

Their charity and caring work is widespread. Joyous music and hymn singing and special celebrations are regular features at the Orsborn Hall while Salvationist holidaymakers from all over the world can be seen amongst the congregation on most Sundays of the year.

Christian Science is based on the teaching of its founder, Mary Baker Eddy, who through faith in the healing powers of God was cured of a serious illness. In thanksgiving the Mother Church was opened in 1879 in Boston, Massachusetts. Services are based on the teachings of Mrs. Eddy and the Bible.

The first public service in Bournemouth was held in Verulam Chambers, Yelverton Road, in July 1906. As membership increased larger premises were obtained. After becoming a society in 1911, the service was formed into a church in 1915. The present building was purchased in 1923 in Christchurch Road and by 1927 the first service was held there. Through its teachings man realises that he was created in the image and likeness of God and that, therefore, material complaints can be overcome by realising this truth. Every Wednesday there is a Testimonial Evening to give thanks for Christ's healing powers.

The Winton Elim Pentecostal Church came into being as the result of a campaign in the 1920s by a Welsh evangelist, George Jeffreys. His preaching was powerful and was accompanied by dramatic healings. In 1926 he and his members erected a marquee in Moordown. Although publicity was minimal, stories of the miraculous healings spread quickly. Soon the tent was overcrowded and people were standing to hear his message. When, after staying longer than was originally planned, the tent was dismantled, the converts needed a church of their own. After meeting in local halls, land was purchased in 1936 in Hawthorn Road, Winton, and the Elim Church was built. (Elim means 'an oasis and place of refreshing'.)

CHAPTER FOUR

# Government

## Self-Government

Before 1856 Bournemouth had no municipal government. Estates were developed by individual landowners and credit has always been given to these enterprising planners. Problems of water supply, sanitation, lighting and the rough condition of muddy, stony roads, all became very urgent. It was obvious that the needs of a developing town could no longer be determined by rural Holdenhurst.

In the words of Mate and Riddle:

Prior to 1856 Bournemouth had less of the privileges of local self-government than the meanest village in the land. The smallest area has its Parish Meeting with the opportunity of public grievances. Bournemouth, before 1856, had not even that. Householders had the right to attend the Vestries at Holdenhurst and Christchurch but the exercise of this privilege meant a long journey.[1]

**39** East beach, c.1875. Bathing became popular, but men and women were strictly segregated. The Undercliff was not constructed until 1907.

The Bournemouth Improvement Act was passed on 14 July 1856 and slowly changed a picturesque watering place into a new town. The Act provided for improved paving, sewerage, draining, lighting and cleaning and other provisions. A restricted area of administration was defined as 'within the radius of a mile whereof the centre is the front door of the Belle Vue Hotel'. The entire area comprised 1,140 acres. Thirteen Commissioners had to be elected of whom the lord of the manor and his nominee were permanent members. Qualification for membership was by owning property of an annual value of £30 and living in the designated area or not more than a mile outside it. The Board included John Tregonwell (son of Lewis Tregonwell), Samuel Bayly (the first proprietor of *Belle Vue Hotel*), and other businessmen.

A rate not exceeding 3s. in the pound was authorised. Thomas Kingdom became the first clerk at a salary of £26 p.a.; he was to attend all meetings, take minutes and accounts. The first Surveyor and Inspector of Nuisances was Christopher Crabbe Creeke, whose duties included the improvement of the surfacing and gravelling of the muddy, unmade roads and the production of a detailed map of the district. He was paid £50 p.a. which was increased to £150 in 1868 out of which he had to pay a foreman and an inspector.

Bournemouth's main services were still in Christchurch, including the relieving officer, the board of guardians, parish doctor, vaccinator, coroner, and the registrar of births and deaths. One of the first advertisements in the *Visitors' Directory*, first published in 1858, was from Mr. Attewell, of Christchurch, a hairdresser and cutter, who announced that he would attend Bournemouth every Tuesday and Friday.

**40**  Upper Pleasure Gardens showing the water tower, *c.*1885, which operated the ornamental fountains. The tower is still there, but the fountains were demolished, *c.*1992.

The Invalids' Walk from the Arcade

**41 & 42** Invalids' Walk. After the First World War the name was changed to Pine Walk. The developing town wished to be associated with visitors and residents and not only with invalids.

**43** The Lower Pleasure Gardens before draining in 1873. At one time horses and cows grazed in the muddy ground. In the left-hand background can be seen the second St Andrew's Presbyterian Church and the studio hut used by Robert Day, the first photographer in Bournemouth.

The Board of Commissioners eagerly set to work, even though they were faced with financial problems which required them to borrow money until the collection of the first rate revenue. After discussions with the Gervis Estate land was transferred to the Commissioners, including Westover Gardens, which were improved by paths and flowerbeds, and the construction of a central walk which led to the *Bath Hotel*, known as Invalids Walk. After the First World War the name was changed to Pine Walk, its present name. Meadowland on either side of the Bourne stream, which consisted of bogs and mire only suitable for horses and cattle, was drained and became the attractive Lower Pleasure Gardens. The first road to be improved was Westover Road, the main residential road, the labourers being paid 12s. a week.

## More Self-Government

In 1882 the Municipal Corporation Act was passed, which allowed certain districts to become municipal boroughs with extended powers of government. It was then suggested that Bournemouth should seek greater authority, which would enable the town to break away from remaining controls exercised by the sprawling parishes of Christchurch and Holdenhurst.

After three attempts a charter was finally approved and received royal assent on 23 July 1890. The Board of Commissioners was replaced by a council of elected councillors and aldermen, together with the creation of wards and the appointment of a town clerk and borough treasurer. A holiday was proclaimed in Bournemouth on 27 August 1890, when the long-awaited charter would be received from London by a delegation who

travelled on a special coach of the South-Western Railway; from the East (later Central) station they rode in an open coach. There was a joyful procession with tableaux and eight bands. At the gaily decorated pier entrance, the Charter of Incorporation was read out by James Druitt, the legal adviser to the commissioners, who was appointed the first town clerk in appreciation of his long and helpful services to the town. A system of secret ballot was introduced for the first time.

T.J. Hankinson, the former chairman of the commissioners, became the first mayor, being rewarded for his outstanding assistance and advice. He had come to Bournemouth in 1858 for health reasons and was soon known as a successful stationer, publisher and estate agent. Adjoining his home, Victoria House, he founded a popular library, the Victoria Library. In 1875 his business was transferred to the foot of Richmond Hill when a series of local guide books were published by him.

A mace and mayoral badge with the name of the first mayor were presented to the council in March 1891 by Merton Russell-Cotes and his wife, and an 18-carat gold chain was paid for and presented by members of the council and the town clerk.

By charter the new authority was allowed to have its own armorial bearings. Shortage of history caused a problem, but as the area of Bournemouth was once a royal demesne of King Edward the Confessor, the College of Arms decided that the arms of the monarch should form the basis of the shield which would consist of a gold cross *fleurie*. In the first and fourth quarters is a lion rampant holding a rose, representing the many battles of the Middle Ages. On the second quarter are six martlets or sand martins and, on the third, four salmons, thus linking the natural life of the district with its new crest. Besides being a royal emblem, the rose was the emblem of the county of Hampshire, in which Bournemouth was then

**44** *Above left*. When Bournemouth achieved municipal borough status in 1890, Merton and Annie Russell-Cotes showed their pleasure by donating a fine mayoral badge, the loop consisting of 18-carat gold.

**45** *Above right*. Bournemouth Coat of Arms.

**46** *Below*. Outside the Town Hall at the Bournemouth Unitary Launch and Celebration Day, 1 April 1997. For 23 years Bournemouth had a reduced status and was taken from Hampshire into Dorset.

situated. Over all is a pine tree under the branches of which are four more roses. Below the shield is the motto *Pulchritudo et Salubritas*, meaning 'beauty and health'.

Rapid developments took place; land was acquired for public parks and open spaces, a public library was formed in Old Christchurch Road and by 1898 mobile libraries visited outlying areas. Problems of cliff erosion existed and in 1903 Sir George Meyrick gave the corporation exclusive rights to build an Undercliff Drive. The opening in 1907 gave particular pleasure to Merton Russell-Cotes, a progressive townsman and an advocate of Undercliff Drive. To honour the occasion he presented to the town his wonderful collection of works of art which he had obtained on his travels throughout the world. At the same time his wife presented their residence, East Cliff Hall (now the Russell-Cotes Art Gallery and Museum), where these valuable items would be housed, with the proviso that they would continue living there until their deaths.

On 28 July 1898, Councillor C. Mate moved that efforts be made to secure complete autonomy by applying to become a county borough, with its own Quarter Sessions and Commission of Peace. Increased status was granted on 1 April 1900. Further extensions took place in 1914 and 1931 including Holdenhurst, despite its opposition. Hengistbury Head, that great mound of antiquity of which Bournemouth is justly proud, was then owned by Gordon Selfridge, who had grandiose plans for constructing a 300-roomed castle. Fortunately for posterity he was unable to carry out his scheme and sold the headland to Bournemouth Council for £25,250. What an achievement! Heath and wasteland had been transformed to a fine, modern, coastal resort in less than a century.

In 1946 Bournemouth suggested the amalgamation of Christchurch, Poole and Bournemouth under one single authority. The scheme was violently opposed, when Bournemouth was likened to an octopus whose tentacles were ready to envelop others.

Local government reorganisation, after discussions for many years, became law in 1974, with the result that Bournemouth County Borough in Hampshire became part of Dorset and its status reduced to that of a borough under the County Council of Dorset in Dorchester. It was not until 1 April 1997, the long-awaited day, arrived when Bournemouth came, once again, an all-purpose Unitary Authority, after 23 years under Dorset County Council.

## CHAPTER FIVE

# Growing Pains

### Joy's Folly

One of the oldest shopping areas is in Commercial Road but in 1863 six modern, larger shops, with accommodation above, were erected by Henry Joy, a carpenter, builder and astute businessman. These splendid buildings at the beginning of Old Christchurch Road were named Southbourne Terrace. Gervis Arcade or Bournemouth Arcade was started in 1866 by Henry Joy, who envisaged a modern arcade which would become a popular shopping precinct. It was soon adversely criticised and known as 'Joy's Folly', especially as it took seven years to complete. It looked more like an avenue and lacked a roof until 1872. It was thought that the venture would be a complete failure, and originally a shop with accommodation could be rented for as little as £40 p.a.

**47**  *Above right*. Gervis Arcade with milk float.

**48**  *Right*. Gervis Arcade. No one thought that it would become a most prestigious part of the centre of Bournemouth.

One of the main objections to Joy's project was because it meant the destruction of a popular beauty spot known as Church Glen. One guide book stated that it would spoil one of the most picturesque spots in Bournemouth. The pretty glen was crossed by a charming rustic bridge built of rough fir poles and covered with ivy and other climbing plants. About 20 feet below the bridge was a tiny brook which flowed into the Bourne stream. The bridge had been erected in 1853 by Thomas Shettle, an original member of the Board and Chairman of the Commissioners from 1861-4, for the benefit of his tenants in Old Christchurch Road; a fee of one halfpenny was charged for its use by other members of the public.

One of the first shops to be opened, in 1871, was a needlework one by Frederick Bright, who had returned from missionary work in India because of poor health. This developed into a high-class department store called Bright's and now known as Dingle's. His son, Percy May Bright, a respected and active citizen, was chosen as mayor from 1929-31. The arcade is now considered one of the most prestigious parts of Bournemouth.

49  Bournemouth Square in 1865.

50  Rustic bridge. There was much opposition to Joy's proposed arcade which meant the destruction of attractive Church Glen and the picturesque rustic bridge.

## We Must Have A Pier

Although Bournemouth was slowly expanding, it lacked an important amenity—a pier, a feature already possessed by many coastal resorts. The urgency was stressed by some of the chief residents who pointed out that when the waves were high it was impossible to approach the shore without being swamped. The pier was actually described in Brannon's *Guide Book* of 1855 although it was not completed until 1856. As money was not available for a 'real' pier, a landing stage was built on wooden piles with a retractable platform. Unfortunately it was damaged by a severe storm that same year and had to be repaired.

In 1861 it was replaced by a wooden pier 800 feet long which was opened with great ceremony on 17 September by Sir George Gervis. There were gun salutes, fireworks, pleasure steamers and a dinner at the *Belle Vue Hotel*. People were delighted, and soon fashionably clad gentlefolk could be seen strolling along the pier while their carriages awaited them at the pier entrance. Soon there was trouble, as within only five years the wooden piles had been attacked by the teredo or ship worm and became so weak that they had to be replaced by cast iron ones. Its T-shaped head was destroyed by a severe gale, shortening the pier by 300 feet. In January 1867 a gale destroyed another 100 feet. The pier was doomed, but it was not until 1880 that a stronger iron pier was constructed. In 1980, the centenary of the last pier, it was decided to replace the badly corroded ironwork with reinforced concrete as part of a new, modern pier. Despite the loss of many seaside piers elsewhere, Bournemouth had decided that such an important amenity must be retained.

**51** The first jetty pier, 1856, had a retractable platform. Because of storm damage it was replaced by a wooden one in 1861 (as shown above). Due to attacks by teredo worm and more storm damage, it was replaced by a stronger one in 1880.

**52** *Above*. The doomed pier, 1870.
Following storm damage the
wooden piles, after attack by teredo
worms, were replaced by cast-iron
piles.

**53** *Above right*. The pier approach
in 1875, from the west.

**54** *Right*. The pier in 1875. Well-
dressed people enjoy the delights of
walking over the sea.

55   The pier approach in 1903.

## We Don't Want a Railway

Although the railway age was developing rapidly, bringing progress and increased population to many seaside resorts, the landowners of Bournemouth opposed the idea of a railway station for over 20 years on the grounds that it was noisy, dirty and would attract a lower class of people to the detriment of Bournemouth's wealthy invalids. A line between Poole and Southampton had existed since 1847 but it completely bypassed Bournemouth, and it was not until 1870 that Bournemouth had its own railway station, when a branch line was extended from Christchurch to Bournemouth. Because of intense opposition it had to be constructed on the very edge of the Commissioners' district in an area of brickworks. It was known as Bourne-

mouth East Station, resulting in a population of 1,707 in 1861 increasing to 5,896 by 1871.

A frequently heard verse dating from those opposition days of about 1863 was:

'Tis well from far to hear the railway scheme,
And watch the curling, lingering clouds of
  steam
But let not Bournemouth's heath's approved
  abode
Court the new presence of the iron road.

When extensions to the line were proposed in 1882 the verse was heard again.

It was not until 1874 that Bournemouth West Station was constructed providing rail travel with the west of England. For 14 years the two stations were unconnected. The station closed entirely in 1965.

**56** Steam trains at Bournemouth Central Station (formerly Bournemouth East Station), 14 April 1939.

**57** Site of Boscombe Railway Station. The station was closed under the Beeching plan.

**58** Steam trains at West Station, 16 March 1963. The station was closed in 1965.

In 1885 a new East Station was constructed on the west side of Holdenhurst Road. A.L. Popplewell wrote in his well researched book *Bournemouth Railway History*, 'What other town would have forced the London & South Western Railway Co. at the height of its power to design its new station to resemble of all things—a Winter Gardens?'

Bournemouth East Station became Bournemouth Central in 1899, its present name.

Whilst Bournemouth could never lay claim to being one of England's great spas, it certainly gained renown in the 1880s and much of that was due to the favourable views expressed by another physician, Dr. Horace Dobell.

CHAPTER SIX

# The Villages

## Boscombe and Springbourne

By 1875 Bournemouth wanted to expand the limited area granted by the Improvement Act of 1856. As Boscombe and Springbourne adjoined its boundary it seemed natural that the first petition for expansion should incorporate them. In 1875 the Commissioners made a request to the Local Government Board for their inclusion. Although the appeal was opposed by Boscombe, the Board assented to their wishes, which increased the sea-front area and gave Bournemouth another 503 acres.

The number of stylish, detached villas in Bournemouth continued to increase but no provision had been made for artisans, plasterers, builders, carpenters and others to work in the new watering place; they were expected to live outside the area. Boscombe and Springbourne became one of these areas, on its north side.

**59** Boscombe beach, looking towards Bournemouth pier, *c*.1895; a few bathing huts but not many people on the beach.

**60**  By 1850, on lonely Boscombe heathland stood a picturesque wayside inn with the strange name of the *Ragged Cat*. It later became the *Palmerston Arms*, in memory of Lord Palmerston.

The name 'Boscombe' has appeared in several forms. During the reign of Queen Elizabeth I reference is made to 'certain mines of alum and copperas in Baskaw'.[1] In state papers of June 1574 it is spelt 'Bastome'.[2] In 1803 it was called 'Boskom'.[3] Boscombe was originally separated from Bournemouth by dense woods and moorland. By 1850 on the lonely Boscombe heathland stood a picturesque wayside inn bearing the strange name of the *Ragged Cat*; it later became the *Palmerston Arms* after Lord Palmerston. (After acquiring a reputation for drunkenness and bad behaviour it became the *Deacon c.*1990.)

The first estate, Boscombe Cottage, comprised 17 acres and was built in 1801 for Philip Norris near the site of the old Copperas House. The building owes its fame to the fact that it was occupied by Sir Percy Florence Shelley (son of the poet Percy Bysshe Shelley), from 1849 for 40 years. (See Chapter Ten.)

To provide workmen's homes, Dr. William Dale Farr, the owner of land in Boscombe, parts of Springbourne and Iford, made land available for building leases, in about 1864 forming a suburb along Cleveland Road (then Princess Road) and Windham Road,

named after Dr. Farr. By about 1880 some fifty houses had been built in the Springbourne area, including a mission chapel, later replaced by St Clement's Church. Over a dozen houses had also been erected along the newly constructed roads in adjoining Boscombe. All the roads were given the names of statesmen; for example, Walpole, Gladstone, Churchill, Salisbury, Palmerston and Ashley.

The growing popularity of Boscombe was due mainly to the foresight of Sir Henry Drummond Wolff, a diplomat and politician who hoped to make Boscombe a rival watering place to Bournemouth. After retiring, he purchased land from Lord Malmesbury mainly on the south side, consisting primarily of pine woods, between Boscombe Chine and Shore Lane (now Sea Road). For himself he built in 1868 a stately villa called Boscombe Towers (now part of the *Burlington Hotel*). In his house was born the Primrose League (given in memory of Disraeli who loved primroses).

The name 'Boscombe Spa' was given to his estate, from the properties of a ferruginous stream near the Chine. The impregnate waters of the small stream were said to be completely pure and mildly chalybeate. Sir Henry erected

**61** *Burlington Hotel* was originally built as a villa—Boscombe Towers—on land acquired between Boscombe Chine and Shore Lane for Sir Henry Drummond Wolff, a diplomat and politician.

**62** Windsor Road, 1892, off Sea Road. It is hard to believe that this tree-filled area now consists of hotels and flats.

a small thatched building around the spring which attracted many visitors from neighbouring Bournemouth to drink the waters. Many of these enthusiasts walked all the way through lonely paths and climbed up steep Boscombe Hill to narrow Boscombe Spa Road (the name given in memory of the spa).

Other villas were built on the estate, some of which he named after personal or literary friends. Sir Algeron Borthwick (later Lord Glenesk), a neighbour and a friend of Sir Henry, was also active in fostering the progress of Boscombe. When he founded a satirical, social-political magazine called *The Owl*, Sir Henry became one of the first subscribers and that is why the unusually named Owls Road was so called. The correct origin of the road is not well known, many people thinking it has something to do with 'our feathered friends'.

In addition, Sir Henry was responsible for laying out Boscombe Chine as gardens and building a bridge across it. The Chine, also known as Boscombe Bunny, was a deep narrow chine, cut by a stream and leading to the sea. Tennis courts were provided and an old brick kiln in the chine was demolished to be replaced by a rustic building for the accommodation of tennis players.

To cater for visitors who came to the area, the *Boscombe Spa Hotel* was built in 1874 (now the *Chine Hotel* and considerably enlarged).

St Clement's, with its majestic, tall tower, was the first parish church to be built in Springbourne. Through the generosity of Edmund Christy, who came to Bournemouth from Aberdeen, a gift of £30,000 was made for the church, vicarage and a school to be

**63**   The foot of Boscombe Hill, 1862, was a very lonely road then. Dense woods separated Boscombe from Bournemouth.

 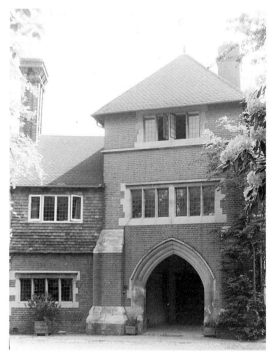

**64**  *Above left.* The Tudor-style home of Edmund Christy, a wealthy bachelor and a devout Christian. The Knole was built in 1873 by his friend, J.D. Sedding, a clever Bristol architect. (It is now a Masonic Lodge.)

**65**  *Above right.* Entrance to the Convent of the Sisters of Bethany, an Anglican religious community founded in 1866—at one time they cared for over 100 orphans.

built. Part of the site of the church was in the same road as his fine Tudor-style home. The Knole was built as a manor house in 1873 by his friend J.D. Sedding, a talented Bristol architect. The Knole became the home of Sir Henry Page Croft, M.P. for Christchurch (1910) and the first M.P. for the Borough of Bournemouth (*c.*1918). Later The Knole became a Masonic Lodge and its museum contains an imposing collection of masonic regalia and information.

Closely associated with St Clement's Church was the Convent of the Sisters of Bethany. A site adjoining St Clement's Church was purchased, then described as part of the untamed moorland of the New Forest. The sisters were asked by Rev. Tinling, the first vicar of St Clement's, to look after children in a small orphanage in the convent; by 1892 there were 105 children in it. By the end of the 1930s the

state had become more responsible for the welfare of orphans and the children were placed elsewhere. This was fortunate as in 1940 a passing German bomber demolished the orphanage wing. By the 1980s the imposing House of Bethany had become too large for the decreasing number of nuns and was sold to Bournemouth Council to provide flats for elderly persons. While it was sad to witness the destruction of magnificent trees in the extensive convent grounds, the housing estate that resulted must have delighted the nuns that their former home and grounds had provided houses and flats for so many local people.

Adjoining Boscombe, the home of Sir Percy Florence Shelley, and extending from Wentworth Road to Fisherman's Walk, Southbourne, was the summer residence and estate of Lord Portman of Bryanston, Blandford. Wentworth Lodge was built *c.*1873 and remained in the family until 1922. The large ornamental drive and the former lodge can still be seen in Christchurch Road, the latter belonging to Deric Scott, Funeral Directors.

The well-constructed Victorian house, with its stables, cobbled yard and walled kitchen gardens was considerably enlarged over a period of years after being purchased by the Collegiate School for Girls in 1899. Dr. J.D. Jones, Minister of Richmond Congregational Church (now United Reformed) from 1898

to 1937, and other Free Church members opened a girls' school to provide a sound Christian education in a house called Towerfield in Poole Road. When the house became too small for the growing school they were able to acquire Wentworth Lodge in 1922 when much of the surrounding estate was sold to finance extensions. Since 1994 the school has been known as Wentworth College, and 1996 marked the 125th anniversary of its foundation.

**66 a-d** *Above left*. Pediment, Walpole Road, Boscombe. *Above right*. Gazebo roof in Walpole Road (similar ones can be seen in various parts of Bournemouth). *Below right*. Clock gable, Christchurch Road. *Below left*. Neck gable, Christchurch Road. Drawings by Harry L. Edwards.

**67** *Above left.* Lady Jane Shelley fixed the first pile of the new Boscombe Pier on 17 October 1888 amidst great jubilation.

**68** *Above right.* The Duke of Argyll who performed the opening ceremony of the new pier in 1889. He stayed at the *Boscombe Spa Hotel* (now the *Chine Hotel*), the first hotel in Boscombe.

## Further Development in Boscombe

Although houses continued to be built, up to 1885 Boscombe remained an outlying district with no railway station and no pier; and piers were a great attraction in the Victorian age. The Commissioners were asked to provide a pier. When they refused Boscombe Pier Co. was formed in 1888 with Sir Henry Drummond Wolff and other prominent persons as directors. The independent attitude of the district and its wish to rival Bournemouth were evident. On 17 October of that year there was jubilation as Lady Jane Shelley fixed the first pile. There were celebrations, decorations and a procession. Gaily-painted notices read 'PROSPERITY TO BOSCOMBE', 'LONG LIVE SIR PERCY AND LADY SHELLEY', 'WELCOME TO OUR VISITORS'.

The opening ceremony was performed by the Duke of Argyll, who stayed at the *Chine Hotel* with his son, the Marquis of Lorne. In his speech the Duke said that, when he was ill in 1846, he was advised to go to Bournemouth, the only place where his health would be improved. When he arrived all he saw was the *Bath Hotel*, a few houses and nothing else. He and his friend took long walks without meeting a single human being. After 10 days his health was restored.

Although it offered roller skating and music, the pier was never a financial success. In 1903 it was purchased by Bournemouth Corporation. It was repaired with a concrete head in 1925, and breached in 1940—along with Bournemouth pier—to prevent enemy landings. The head and neck were repaired in concrete in 1957-8.

Further developments took place mainly due to the progressive outlook of Archibald Beckett, the Boscombe representative for the ward. He was responsible for the erection of the *Salisbury Hotel* in 1890, the arcade in 1892 and the theatre in 1895. Since Bournemouth had a pier, arcade and theatre, Boscombe must

**69**  Boscombe Pier, 1897. Despite several activities, it was never very profitable.

**70**  Boscombe Pier Approach, 1903.

**71**  Boscombe Arcade, 1902. An organ used to play several times daily from a gallery overlooking the arcade.

have them too. The magnificent L-shaped glass edifice was named the Royal Boscombe Arcade. It had two entrances, one in Christchurch Road and one in Palmerston Road, and cost over £40,000 to build. The 1,000-guinea organ was played daily at 11.30 a.m. whilst orchestral concerts were given at 3.30 p.m. Until about 1930 shoppers could also listen to pleasant music in an arcade often adorned with palms and cacti.

The Grand Pavilion Theatre, also known as the Boscombe Theatre cost £16,000. The superb building was luxuriously furnished and could accommodate 3,000 people. There were three tiers of balconies, three private boxes, two buffets and two smoking lounges. Boxes were 15s. and balcony seats 9d. and 6d. Dramatic and musical performances were given daily. Many well-known artistes performed at the theatre including Henry Irving, Ellen Terry, Sarah Bernhardt and Lillie Langtry.

On the opposite side of Christchurch Road, facing the theatre, a large devil still leers down at passers-by. It was erected as a sign of protest by those who were horrified at the thought of bawdy or improper musical or dramatic perform-ances and who wished for a church to be established there. Some residents had even knelt down on the pavement in prayer against the opening of the theatre. Because their attempts had been unsuccessful, the devil was erected. Underneath was inscribed, 'The devil comes into his own' (no longer legible), and the date 1896.

After the theatre had been closed for a time it was re-opened in February 1905 as a music hall called The Hippodrome. Artistes included Marie Lloyd, Vesta Tilley, Hetty King, David Nixon, Harry Tate and Eric Jones-Evans, a local celebrity. The Hippodrome was closed in 1956 to become the Royal Arcade ball-room, Tiffany's. In 1982 it became a night-club, The Academy. By then the interior had become shabby. The new owners renovated and restored the dance room to its original décor of gold and cream paint, but with more modern equipment and lasers.

## Westbourne

Bournemouth increased its boundaries for the second time, in August 1884, with the inclusion of Westbourne and other districts.

Westbourne is one of the most elegant parts of fashionable Bournemouth. Despite the disappearance of many fine Victorian villas which have been replaced by uninteresting flats, there is still an atmosphere of gracious living. In Seamoor Road, formerly the Crescent, is the splendid arcade constructed in 1884 by Henry Joy, similar in style to the one he built in 1866 in the centre of Bournemouth. Proud of his second arcade, Joy had his name and construction date 1884 engraved in large letters by both the Poole Road and the Seamoor Road entrances. High up, at the head of drainpipes are 22 amusing gargoyles who leer and grin at shoppers below. Joy used to live at Seamoor House (demolished), near the Arcade giving Seamoor Road its name.

72  The elegant arcade in Westbourne—created by Henry Joy in 1884. I wonder how many people have seen the gargoyles leering at them.

73  Alum Chine, Bournemouth. There were no high rise flats then, c.1946.

In the 19th century, Westbourne consisted of wild heathland; thick gorse bushes covered the sandy cliffs. There were densely wooded chines or ravines, frequented by smugglers who found good hiding places for their contraband. In 1860 there were only about six houses in the whole area. Its development was due mainly to the expansion of three estates which were purchased on the death of Miss Bruce, who owned the extensive Branksome Estate which stretched from the sea front, along Poole Road to Talbot Woods.

The Alum Cliff Estate was purchased by R. Kerley for building plots. Branksome Dene, a fine Victorian mansion, was the first villa on the site, erected in 1860 for C.A. King. In the Sydenham *Guide* of 1887 it was described as standing to the west of Alum Chine on a fine

**74** The pedestrian gate which used to be by the entrance to The Avenue, marking the boundary between Bournemouth and Poole, has been re-erected in Leicester Road, behind a bowling green.

site commanding beautiful views and illustrating how the wild heath can be rapidly brought into a state of 'luxuriant cultivation'. Rather surprisingly he continues,

> ... the mansion is a square pile with little architectural pretension but well planned and spacious. The lodge [still in Alumhurst Road] stables and watertower are very pretty structures and there is a picturesque rustic bridge across one of the gorges of unusual design.

The Dower House in Alumhurst Road has been the Chine Breeze Nursing Home for some time and opposite is the Old Lodge where the coachman once lived.

There was also the Consolidated Land Society and the Branksome Tower Estate, most of which was just outside the Bournemouth boundary. It was purchased by C.W. Packe, M.P., who in 1855 built the picturesque Branksome Towers (now a block of flats). The Avenue, famous for its wonderful rhododendrons and stylish villas, was originally a private road leading to Branksome Towers. There was a lodge and iron gates which were known as 'County Gates' marking the boundary between Poole and Bournemouth. From 1890 to the 1970s the Lodge was occupied by Rebbecks, Estate Agents, but when they left the lodge was demolished; the small pedestrian gate was removed and has since been completely rebuilt in Leicester Road behind a bowling green.

There was enmity, resulting in litigation, between Mr. King and Mr. Packe when the latter had a rustic bridge and an embankment erected in his part of the chine, which blocked Mr. King's sea view. But the embankment has long since gone. Charles Packe died in 1867 and, together with his wife, Kitty, who died later, is buried in a large, stone mausoleum by the entrance of Branksome Dene Chine. Another nine shelves were intended for other members of the family, who did not choose to be buried in the gloomy building. For many years the mausoleum has looked shabby and vandalised, until a few years ago it was restored and re-consecrated by Poole Council.

**75** Branksome Dene, erected in 1860. It was originally owned by C.A. King and later by Sir Ernest Cassel, grand-father of Edwina Ashley Mountbatten. (Now Zetland Court, a Masonic retirement home.)

**76** Canford Manor, the former home of Lord and Lady Wimborne. It has been a well-known public school for many years.

Branksome Dene was later occupied by Sir Ernest Cassel (grandfather of Edwina Ashley Mountbatten), who didn't feel able to maintain it, and sold much of the area. It was then purchased by Lord Wimborne of Canford Manor as a holiday residence. Lady Wimborne was the sister of Lord Randolph Churchill and in 1892, when the Churchills spent the winter months there, Winston, then 18 years old, nearly lost his life. He was chased by his younger brother and cousin and, to escape capture, he climbed a fir tree and fell 29ft. to the ground; he was unconscious for three days and confined to his bed for three months. How the history of the world could have been changed! From 1934 to 1947 Branksome Dene became a 'Vegetarian Hotel', when a visitor wrote of the Italian garden and rock garden, 'A reproduction of a Mediterranean view on the English Channel. The sea is near and murmurs—as the pines—truly the Harmony of Nature'.

During the Second World War it was occupied by members of the Board of Education and then became a Jewish Convalescent Home, when a room could be obtained for ten guineas a week and with FULL BOARD! By that time much work needed to be done on the building and, when it was purchased in 1983 by the Royal Masonic Benevolent Institution for retired Masons, it was completely restored and refurbished and now reveals the splendour of its early days. It is known as Zetland Court after the Earl of Zetland, a Grand Master of the Royal Masonic Benevolent Institution for 26 years, and gives happiness and pleasure to the lucky occupants.

Still in Alumhurst Road is the Herbert Hospital, built in 1865 as a memorial to Lord Sidney Herbert of Lea. He was a close friend of Florence Nightingale, of Embley Park near Romsey, and as Secretary for War he was responsible for her going out to Scutari to nurse during the Crimean War. A Report issued in 1867 stated that

> a commodious edifice has risen at Bournemouth on a noble site, facing the sea where the patients will possess the advantages of pure and healthy air. The design was furnished by Miss Nightingale, a lady who was qualified to know of the best mode of treating the sick. She insisted that the patients were in detached wings instead of being concentrated in one block. She insisted that every window was designed to catch the sun and all rooms had to be light and airy.

Although in ill health, Florence expected to be consulted at all stages. Today the original

**77** Nightingale House, the original part of Herbert Hospital.

**78** Robert Louis Stevenson who lived in Bournemouth from 1884-87. Although ill much of the time, he wrote there his best-seller, *The Strange Case of Dr. Jekyll and Mr. Hyde*, and other books.

**79** Mrs. R.L. Stevenson, described by Louis as his wife, lover, friend and best critic.

building, Gothic in style and built of Purbeck stone, is called Nightingale House, while the whole complex with many new buildings still bears the name of Herbert Hospital. The building now cares for those mentally handicapped, those suffering from mental illness—and there are special flats for those who are able to manage on their own in sheltered accommodation. Lord Herbert and Florence Nightingale would be proud of the advanced caring work that takes place in Herbert Memorial Hospital.

Leading off Seamoor Road is R.L. Stevenson Avenue (formerly Middle Road) which commemorates Robert Louis Stevenson who lived nearby from 1884 to 1887 in a house called Sea View which had been given to his wife by her father-in-law. The name was changed to Skerryvore to honour their family firm who had constructed the lighthouse

Skerryvore off the Argyll coast. Although Stevenson was ill, he wrote, whilst in Bournemouth, *A Child's Garden of Verse* evoking memories of his childhood, and *Kidnapped*, and, by contrast, his immediate best-seller, *The Strange Case of Dr. Jekyll and Mr. Hyde*. In his own words, 'he lived like a weevil in a biscuit', but he had time for a few special friends, mainly Sir Percy and Lady Shelley of Boscombe Manor. He died in 1894 after settling in Samoa in the South Seas. Skerryvore was practically destroyed by bomb damage in November 1940 and was demolished the following year despite appeals for its restoration as a historic building. In 1954 Bournemouth Corporation acquired the site for a memorial garden when the outline of the house was laid out in stone and a small stone lighthouse, a copy of the one off the Argyll coast, was erected.

## Winton and Other Small Districts

In 1901 Bournemouth (by then a county borough), increased its boundaries again to include Winton, Moordown, Pokesdown, Southbourne and Richmond Park, which were formerly in the parish of Holdenhurst. By then it had a population of 59,762 and comprised 5,850 acres.

Winton commenced as an area for artisans as did Boscombe, Springbourne and Pokesdown. The name 'Winton' was unknown until the mid-19th century when the land consisted of wild heathland, including Wallis Down (now Wallisdown) and Moor Down (Moordown). The area was described as

> ... intersected by tracks of carts in which peat, then almost the only fuel used, was taken to outlying farms ... away from the main road was the sinister form of gallows, the chains in which the bodies of those who had suffered on it and the ground beneath strewn with the blackened bones of early victims ...[4]

**80**  Georgina Talbot, founder of Talbot Village, which became a home and sanctuary for many poor people.

The earliest known building was in Moordown, a small mud and thatch farmhouse erected by Lewis Tregonwell on land he purchased on the east side of Wimborne Road. The farm was known for its hospitality which, in the early days, extended to the free traders or smugglers. In the late 19th century it was known as Burt's Farm, David Burt living there in 1878 and George Burt, a cowkeeper, from 1911. As time passed it was surrounded by buildings and houses and owned by various retail establishments.

Development of the district was mainly due to the progressive outlook of the Misses Georgina and Marianne Talbot, wealthy philanthropists, who with their family left their London home c.1850 for the newly developed watering town of Bourne. They lived at Hinton Wood House on the East Cliff (demolished and replaced by flats).

There was extreme poverty and crowds of poor people used to stand under their windows calling, 'Give us work, we are starving'. Georgina, whose social conscience was stirred decided to do something. She rented land on the moors from Sir George Gervis and William Driver to provide agricultural work for some of the poor. David Tuck, a farmer, was put in charge of the scheme. The idea of a self-supporting village developed from this trial venture.

Land was purchased with grazing rights for animals of cottagers. The estate included six farms and 16 cottages—another was added in 1872 for the organist of St Mark's Church. The cottages were detached, well constructed, each on one acre of land with its own garden. There was a well and a pigsty and rents ranged from 4s. to 7s. per week. The village was designed for those who were prepared to work to maintain themselves and their families. The sale of poultry, eggs and bacon was permitted and if they became wealthy they were expected to leave to make way for other poor people. The village was based on the precepts 'Love God, Keep the Commandments and Honour the Queen'.

**81 & 82** Talbot Village School, erected in 1862—and plaque.

In 1862 seven attractive almhouses designed by Christopher Crabbe Creeke were constructed of Portland stone for the old and infirm of the labouring classes, thus providing them with peace and security in old age. There were flower and vegetable gardens, an ornamental well, pigsties and a space for poultry, for those whose health permitted them to maintain such animals.

A village school was erected in 1862 consisting of a spacious school-room. It commenced with 68 children with lessons in reading, writing, arithmetic and religious instruction, and in needlework for the girls. A deed of settlement of 1883 granted the sum of £66 'so long as the portrait of Georgina Talbot shall be hung in the schoolroom'. With the passing of the Education Act 1944 the school became grant-aided, but the beautiful portrait still has its place of honour in the school.

By 1870 St Mark's Church, built of Portland and Purbeck stone at a cost of £5,000, had been practically completed. (A new porch added in 1969 cost as much as the original building.) No services were allowed after night-fall over the lonely heath. Unfortunately Georgina died shortly before the consecration of the church and was the first to be buried in the spacious churchyard.

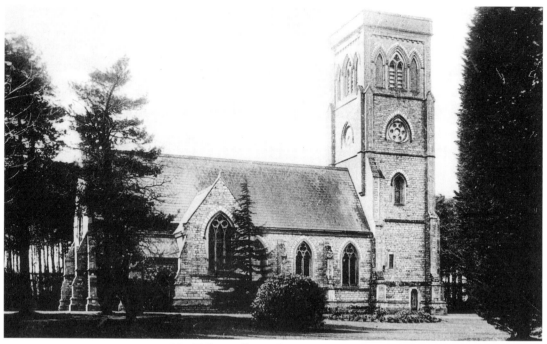

**83**   Talbot Village Church, Wallisdown.

An inscription round the fine Ionic Cross reads:

> She came of an ancient race and possessed of herself that nobility of mind which delighted in the happiness of her fellow creatures. In the neighbourhood of this village she passed 25 years of blameless life giving time and fortune to bettering the conditions of the poorer classes, seeking to minister to their temporal and spiritual welfare, and erecting habitations suitable to their position in life, herself enjoying a peaceful and happy existence in doing good, awaiting the end.

After Georgina's death, her sister, Marianne arranged for the completion of the church and added, as gifts, a gracefully proportioned pulpit, an ancient font procured by their father, Sir George Talbot, at Rome, an organ and church furniture, including two Chippendale chairs which came from the Talbot home. For many years Marianne continued the policy adopted by her sister, which allowed access to the beautiful Talbot woods. Marianne died on 3 November 1885 and another

memorial cross was erected, the inscription extolling her kind and affectionate nature, and her love of beauty and goodness which endeared her through her long and excellent life to her many friends.

After the Misses Talbot had developed their own estate, they purchased land along the main Wimborne Road where they built four-square artisans' cottages and public wells for the supply of water. The Talbots were of Scottish descent of which they were very proud. They named the new settlement 'Winton' after their kinsman, the Earl of Winton (formerly Earl of Eglinton). Many roads were named after Scottish towns and personalities.

As building work progressed, more labourers were attracted to the area, leading to a demand for more houses. The brickmaking industry increased and also that of excavating gravel and clay. The slopes and hollows which the latter caused formed the roads of Calvin, Luther and Cranmer and other roads between Winton and Charminster. There were brick kilns in Claypit

Common. White clay was much in evidence in the district and many of the early cottages were built of this distinctive material. The cottages were built mainly during the 1890s for £140 and could be rented for 4s. 6d. to 5s. 6d. a week.

Spiritual and educational development was the concern of Rev. Morden Bennett, the first vicar of St Peter's Church. After its establishment he turned his attention to the area of Moordown where artisans and agricultural workers were separated from the parish church by two miles of heathland. A mission church was started in a farm cottage in 1851 and in 1853 Sir George Tapps-Gervis gave a plot of land for a permanent chapel school. The building was dedicated to St John in the Wilderness. A new and larger St John's was constructed. In 1873 the foundation was laid by the Earl of Malmesbury when a new parish was also created comprising Winton, Moordown, Redhill and Muscliff. Further schools were also built.

In 1894 Winton became a parish council and in 1897 urban status was granted. There were still problems of drainage and lack of water supply, particularly in Moordown where a horse and cart was used to carry water. There were problems of refuse and emptying cesspools. It was thought that it would be more beneficial to all concerned if Winton was incorporated into Bournemouth where nearly all the artisans worked. In 1901 when Bournemouth gained county borough status Winton and other districts were incorporated into Bournemouth.

## Kinson

Traces of Palaeolithic man have been found in the ancient village of Kinson which lies on the northern boundary of Bournemouth and was one of the last villages to be added to the growing town, when it was taken from Poole. Early records reveal its original name; Cynestanstun from 'tun', a farm of Cynestan, a Saxon chief. Other versions include 'Kynestanton' and 'Kynston'; followed in the 19th century by 'Kingston' and then 'Kinson'.

Unfortunately many of the fine buildings have been demolished. Among them was Howe Lodge, an elegant 18th-century house built by the smuggler, Gulliver. Despite protests, it was demolished in 1958 for road widening and the erection of flats, at which time a concealed room and brick tunnel were discovered. Next door was 'Woodlands', its original parts dating to the 1700s, with thick cob walls and period windows (also demolished), as was Kinson House, at one time the home of the great uncle and aunt of the actress Sybil Thorndyke and her brother Russell. The oldest parts were again said to be linked with smugglers, resulting in Russell writing a book about a clergyman smuggler.

A village green was established in 1968 where two thatched cottages used to be near an old horse pond. A sign (disappeared) stated, 'Any person causing damage to any part of the village green may be liable to chastisement by being placed in the village stocks'; the stocks are still there.

For many years village life centred around the church of St Andrew's. It is of Saxon origin, although only the tower foundations remain from this period. Its Norman tower was constructed of ironstone rubble surmounted by a crenellated parapet. At one time the cover of the 13th-century font of Purbeck marble had to be locked, both to prevent its use for black magic and also during a period of interdiction during the reign of King John. The smugglers' table tomb, where contraband goods were hidden, bore the false names, Jane and William Oakley, 1718 and 1724.

The elegant Georgian building in white stucco with two Tuscan columns, called Pelhams, built in 1793, was once owned by Gulliver. In the late 19th century it became the vicarage and was owned by the Rev. A.M. Sharp until 1930, when he sold the house and park to the council at a moderate price on condition that it was used for the benefit of Kinson people.

There are several historic public houses in Kinson: the *Dolphin* inn, now *Gulliver's Tavern*, which was thought to be a 17th-century coaching inn; the *Travellers' Rest*, until 1840, became the *Royal Oak* in 1863 and was a halting place for travellers, the *Thatched House* in East Howe Lane used to be a pretty *cottage ornée*, c.1820, now a public house.

In 1895 Kinson became a parish council under Dorset County Council and Poole Rural District Council. In 1931 Bournemouth decided to make its final major boundary extension which was to include Kinson, East and West Howe, Ensbury and Talbot Village, all of which were part of the rural district of Poole. There was strenuous opposition, particularly to the 'poaching' of land from another county. Finally, the Kinson residents decided that there were more advantages in incorporation into Bournemouth to which it was becoming more allied. In taking in Kinson the town increased its size by two-thirds to 11,270 acres. The extension also took in Holdenhurst, the 'mother' of Bournemouth: the fashionable young adult thus swallowed its ancient, countrified mother.

## Pokesdown

Pokesdown originally was one of several Saxon agricultural communities in the fertile plains and valleys of the River Stour. Apart from a few cottages and an isolated farm, it was surrounded by uninhabited heaths and dense woods. The name 'Pokesdown' could be a corruption of Pooksdown, while 'pokes' was the smugglers' word for elves. In 1664 an old receipt refers to '1s. from Henry Mantle of Poxdowne'.

The first house to be built between Christchurch and Poole was Stourfield House, constructed in 1766 in Georgian style on a hillock amidst heather and moorland for Edmund Bott, barrister and J.P. He was a man of great intellect who wrote a commentary on the Poor Laws and whose house became a centre for literary discussions. His affection for his moorland home was so great that after his death in 1788 local folk claimed that they had seen him driving his coach and four along the narrow tracks nearby.

After he died the house and estate were purchased by Sir George Tapps who leased it to a number of tenants. The first was the Countess of Strathmore, one of the richest heiresses in England (and an ancestor of the Queen Mother) who was loved and respected for her kindness to the poor of the district. Before she died in 1800 she requested that she be buried in her court dress with a silver trumpet by her side so that she would be able to answer the heavenly trumpeter on Judgement Day. She was buried in Westminster Abbey. The large estate provided employment for Pokesdown's increasing population. In 1844 it was purchased by Admiral William Popham and his family until the estate was broken up in 1893.

To return to the small agricultural community living in Pokesdown in 1820 a weekly prayer meeting was started under the auspices of Christchurch Congregation Church, led by the Rev. Daniel Gunn; it was held in a thatched cottage. By 1834 more permanent premises were needed and a Mr. Troke offered part of his garden for a site. A mud-and-thatch chapel was constructed entirely by the local people. In 1850 Elias Lane, a deacon, became the first pastor of Pokesdown where he worked for the next 20 years. Due to the success of the chapel a larger site of 27 acres became necessary in Hampden and Victoria Roads (now Stourvale and Southbourne Roads), purchased in 1855 at a cost of £1,000.

Elias Lane retired in 1870. The Rev. Elijah Pickford, who suffered from bronchitis, had been advised to leave the north of England for a milder climate. He felt that the hand of God was shown when he was invited to supply pulpit for two Sundays in Pokesdown (where he stayed for the rest of his life). Of his first day he wrote, 'I found myself in a NEW world. Flowers were blooming in the open air and the atmosphere was warm and genial.' When he left home in Lancashire there was more than two feet of snow all around. He continued, that, when he first came to Pokesdown, he was struck by the sparseness of the population as he had lived for a long time in densely crowded localities. According to the census of 1871 there were only 511 inhabitants in Pokesdown, most of whom were artisans working in the building trade and a few worked on local farms. There was only one shop which sold practically everything, but if you wanted a doctor, a lawyer or the signature of a magistrate you had to walk to either Bournemouth or Christchurch as there were no omnibuses or 'brakes'. He continued: 'In those days I walked from Pokesdown to the Lansdowne on a footpath under the shade of pines and I have not met half a dozen people all the way.'

When an Anglican church was required, land was given by Sir George Gervis in 1858 and dedicated to St James the Greater. It was described as one of the most beautiful churches in the county. A school was opened in 1857. A charge of 1d. a week was made for each child and 4d. per family. There were 49 children on the roll.

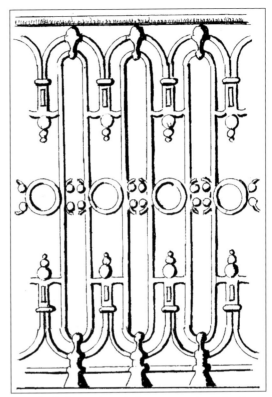

**84** Typical cast-iron balcony seen in Pokesdown and Boscombe, *c*.1890.

**85** Lansdowne Crescent, *c*.1870.

**86** A steam train—an up express, *Sir Bedivere*, passing the 'Pokesdown for Eastern Bournemouth' station board, *c*.1959.

Several unsuccessful attempts had been made to secure a railway station at Pokesdown but it was not until 1883 that the existing line from Christchurch to Bournemouth was extended to include a small station at Pokesdown. For some strange reason it was known as Boscombe station until that district had its own station in 1897 in Ashley Road. (This was discontinued under the Beeching plan, *c*.1966.)

As many children left school at 12 years of age, it was felt that education in science and technical subjects was required for the children of the increasing number of artisans in the district. The foundation stone for an art and technical school was laid in 1898 at the corner of Hannington Road and filled the needs for further education until the opening of the Municipal College at the Lansdowne in 1913.

Towards the end of the 19th century Pokesdown's residents were dissatisfied with the poor condition of unmade roads, lack of main drainage and inadequate street lighting and they asked for incorporation into Bournemouth Borough. Owing to lack of action the district became first a parish, and then in 1895 an Urban District when they were able to deal with some of their problems.

Bournemouth continued to grow and in July 1900 it succeeded in an application for complete independence from Hampshire County Council. In 1901 Pokesdown, with a population then of 5,550, had become part of Bournemouth. While most ratepayers supported amalgamation with the borough, some dissentients thought it a pity that in future no one would know that Pokesdown had had its own council and that its members had acted with enthusiasm to improve their own district.

## Southbourne

Although Southbourne was incorporated into Bournemouth together with Pokesdown in 1901, it has always retained its own character. Originally the area consisted of desolate land in the much older parish of Pokesdown and the name Southbourne was unknown. Nearby were the small agricultural communities of Iford, Wick and Tuckton. The terrain was often referred to as 'The Guns', as gunnery was practised there by coastguards. There were two estates in the area, Stourwood and Stourcliffe, Cellar's Farm and three small stone cottages.

While Bournemouth's commencement was partly due to Dr. Granville, who recommended it as a watering place for the delicate, and Dr. Dobell, who introduced the Mont Dore treatment—it was a third physician, Dr. Thomas A. Compton, whose Bournemouth practice started in 1866, who realised that the pines, wasteland, sandhills and the bracing sea breezes due to its position near the cliff tops, would be most suitable as a health resort. In 1870 he purchased 230 acres of land with one mile of sea frontage for £3,000 and named the district Southbourne-on-Sea. The area was bounded on the west by a sandy track, formerly used by smugglers, and now part of Clifton Road.

A single path led to the sea through Clifton Road, known locally as Mount Misery, perhaps because of the difficulty in climbing down the rocky cliffs, but generally thought to be named as the result of the suicide of a young girl who, after signalling from the cliffs to her smuggler lover to bring his vessel inshore, witnessed, to her horror, the wrecking of the boat and the drowning of her future husband and his mates. Distraught and heartbroken, she threw herself over the cliffs.

Nearby is Fisherman's Walk, where fishermen followed the narrow path to their favourite fishing place below the cliffs. At low tide they trudged wearily back along the path to the *New Bell* inn, the only pub for several miles.

Foxholes was the first house to be built in the new area. In 1872, Henry Reeves, leader-writer of *The Times* and editor of the *Edinburgh Review*, bought a site at Foxholes for his home in retirement. He was not, however, able to live there until 1876. Soon he was writing to his publisher, 'I enjoy my life here beyond all things. Four months have skipped by in this Olympian calm between the sea and sky'.

A few years after Mr. Reeves' death in 1895, Foxholes became a well-known girls' school. As the school grew in size a new wing

**87** Foxholes, the first house to be built in Southbourne.

was added, the difference in style and architecture being easily discernible. In 1937 the school was purchased by Galleon World Travel Association as a hotel. Visitors often commented on the style of the building, which on the southern side was reminiscent of Italy, and also of its curious bas-reliefs in the lounge which were replicas of the Elgin Marbles in the British Museum.

Later it was owned by other hotel proprietors, but in March 1983, due to high costs and fewer visitors, the hotel and contents were sold by auction and the hotel was demolished—another historic building had been destroyed. Appreciative remarks were made about the Elgin Marbles. Several buyers wanted

**88** Replica of one of the Elgin Marbles on the lounge walls at Foxholes. It seems a great pity that they could not be saved.

to purchase them, but the problem of their removal from the walls, undamaged, proved too great. Finally no one had them, and, like the building, they were broken up and destroyed, to be replaced by a large block of flats, in a superb position and with a superb view.

By 1874 Southbourne had its own Winter Gardens built almost entirely of glass and about four years before Bournemouth had its first Winter Gardens. They were situated on the south side of Belle Vue Road near the present Southbourne Crossroads. The Winter Gardens were well-heated and filled with flowers, plants and palms. People from Bournemouth flocked to visit and willingly paid the 6d. entrance fee.

The story behind the Gardens is intriguing as the whole structure was transferred from Tedworth Park, near Andover. Tedworth Park was the home of Assheton Smith, a well-known sportsman, who was disturbed to hear from their physician that he should take his wife to Madeira for the winter for about six months to cure her chest complaint.

As a keen huntsman with his own racing stud, he had no wish to leave England for so long. To avoid leaving England he would bring Madeira to her. He ordered the erection of a huge glass conservatory in the Park which he filled with roses and other flowers, maintaining a temperature of 60° Fahrenheit. There his wife, who was also a keen horsewoman, could have her daily rides in the atmosphere of the warm Mediterranean. After the death of Assheton Smith, the structure was eventually sold, demolished, and then rebuilt in Southbourne.

The nearest church was either the Priory at Christchurch or St James at Pokesdown. In 1876 a small, brick building which served as a school and as a church was erected. It was surrounded by high, straggling gorse bushes and rabbits scampered everywhere. The first verger was John Barnes, who was paid 10s. a quarter to ring the bell and to see to the paraffin lamps. For almost 100 years members of the Barnes family devotedly served the church as vergers. In 1882 the present St Katharine's Church was erected on land donated to the parish by Dr. Compton. The church was named to celebrate the memory of St Katharine, a devout Christian, who was tied to a wheel with sharp knives, but the knives came apart and cut her executioners. The wheel, the emblem of purity, is depicted in the church. In 1881 the Tuckton Bridge Co. was founded by Dr. Compton, who ordered the construction of the original wooden bridge to enable easier access to Christchurch. Until 1943 it was a toll bridge with charges of 6d. for four-wheeled vehicles, ½d. for bicycles and prams and 1d. for pedestrians. In 1904 the bridge was purchased by Bournemouth Borough and replaced by a stronger structure which enabled trams to cross it *en route* for Christchurch.

It was a great occasion when Southbourne had its own pier, built in 1881 at a cost of £4,000 of iron and with a concrete entrance. On 28 December 1900 it was severely damaged by gales and then further demolished by another gale six days later. In 1907, completely derelict, it was dismantled by Bournemouth Corporation as being dangerous. Six three-storey houses built on the Undercliff in 1888, in one of which Dr. Compton lived, had also to be destroyed owing to severe flooding.

The first boys' school in the area, Pembroke Lodge House School was opened in May 1880, commencing with two pupils and increasing to about thirty boys. The fine Victorian building occupied an area in Belle Vue Road near Seafield Road. In 1936 the school moved to Fordingbridge.

The first girls' school, Grassendale, was started over a shop by Miss Tucker and then moved over a newly-built house in Belle Vue Road. In 1888, needing more accommodation, they took larger premises (now St Peter's School) in St Catherine's Road and in 1936 they moved to the site vacated by Pembroke Lodge and changed the name to St Mary's Gate. Their previous school in St Catherine's Road was purchased in 1936 by the Jesuits as a boys' Catholic school and in 1947 by the De La Salle Brothers. The school has been greatly extended since the Grassendale days. (In 1980 the school, the only comprehensive school in Bournemouth, opened its doors to both boys and girls.) Over the door of one of the original buildings was engraved the following:

> Come in with Love, stay long,
> Then bid farewell in peace.

After a severe accident to the last headmistress, Mrs. Kathleen Cook, the school was closed, demolished and became a block of flats, known as St Mary's Court. A sad ending to a very fine school.

**89** Southbourne Pier was built in 1881 at a cost of £4,000. The pier was damaged by gales and was demolished *c.*1907.

90   Thatched cottages at Iford. They were destroyed *c.*1929, due to the (so-called) development of the area.

## Iford

A busy suburb on the eastern boundary of Bournemouth, Iford was originally the site of a ford. In 1150 it was written as 'Huver'. During the 12th to 14th centuries it was 'Huvre' and 'Luvre' but by 1756 it was written as 'Iforde' and also as 'Ifford'.

The ancient bridge dates back to the 12th century and possibly before then. Before the construction of the bridge it was the only means of getting to and from Christchurch for the farming community living along the banks of the river. Until the Statute of Bridges in 1530 the building and maintenance of bridges was regarded as the duty of the local people using them, and their repair was the duty of the county or borough.

Up to the 20th century Iford remained a rustic community with thatched cottages, the blacksmith and wheelwright, a few farms, the *New Inn* and Iford House.

Iford House stood alone in three acres of ground adjoining Castle Lane East and Christchurch Road. The house was built in 1795 for Dr. William Dale Farr, who had land in Iford and Springbourne. It eventually became the property of Dr. Farr's grandson, after whom Windham Road, Springbourne was named. By 1936 it was demolished.

Almost opposite was Iford Farm, managed by the Ellison family. They had numerous pigsties, a stable for farm horses and about seventy cows, all milked by hand. When the last farmer, William Alfred Ellison, died in 1919, mourned and greatly respected, he was carried to his funeral on one of his own farm wagons drawn by two horses. Shortly afterwards the farm changed to dairy farming and by 1931 the building was demolished.

Then there was Clingan's Charity Farm, established under the will of John Clingan of Christchurch who died *c.*1716, for the benefit of poor children of the parish of Christchurch and to apprentice them for sea service. When the farm was demolished in the 1930s, the Trustees allowed Miss Harvey, who had managed the farm alone after her father's death in 1907, to take anything from the farm to her new home. They were more than surprised when she decided to take the front and back doorsteps so that she would continue to cross the same thresholds, and also the flagstones from the hall and dairy floor for her garden paths.

It was greatly regretted that the little village with its thatched houses and pretty gardens had disappeared by *c.*1929 due to the development of the area and the need for a new bridge to take increasing traffic. Taylor Dyson, historian, wrote: 'it was vandalism to sweep away the old cottages even though progress demanded a new bridge'.[5]

## Wick

Wick was originally named, 'Wic' (Old English for a village or dairy farm) and was first mentioned in *c*.1100. 'Week' was used in the Christchurch Inclosure Award of 1805. Whilst not far from the ceaseless traffic on the busy Stour Road, it has retained its village atmosphere of peace and quietness.

Its main focal point is the tiny triangular green which hides the site of an old village well which used to be covered by a trap door. Wick House, formerly the local manor house, was constructed in the Queen Anne period about 1691. It was occupied by John Sloman and his descendants from 1813 to 1939 when it was turned into four terraced maisonettes. It is said that Nelson stayed there, while a subterranean passage was discovered leading to the crypt of Christchurch Priory—probably another of the smugglers' secret underground routes.

Next to Wick House is Wick Farm, which was originally the property of Sir George Tapps and then of his descendants. Prior to 1777 it was known as Knaptons or Holloways, and after that date it became Wick Farm.

Behind the green are the quaint semi-detached houses known as Quality and Tranquillity, the latter, by mistake, becoming the village shop for a short period. Since then there has never been a church, shop or inn in the village. In 1908 the stylish Well House was built, at the back of which was an old barn where church services were held until 1961.

**91** Wick and its tiny, triangular-shaped green, under which is the site of an old village well.

**92** Wick House, *c*.1691. A subterranean passage, another of the smugglers' underground routes, used to lead to the crypt of Christchurch Priory.

To the left of the green is another well-constructed, attractive house, The Sanctuary, behind which was an older cottage and a barn with the date. '1846' engraved in its brickwork. In 1985 it became Wick Farm Estate and an area where fine, modern houses were built, but the date still remains in the brickwork.

Laurel is the tiniest of the 'listed' buildings, erected in 1851. Until the early 20th century an old, thatched 'one-up one-down' cottage was joined to it, known as 'Uncle Tom's Cabin', at one time being occupied by the O'Brien family. John O'Brien was the first pier-master of the ill-fated Southbourne Pier.

The only remaining thatched cottage in Wick, built *c.*1699, was once the home of William Guard, Chief Bo'sun of HMS *Victory*. Later it was owned by his grand-daughter who is mainly remembered for the several monkeys she kept as pets. A seat nearby is inscribed 'In memory of Anna' but few people know that Anna was a monkey.

A ferry has existed in Wick for centuries and water transport has always played an important part in the life of the villagers. Before Tuckton Bridge was constructed in 1882, the only other route to Christchurch was by Iford Lane and Old Iford Bridge.

## Tuckton

The tiny hamlet of Tuckton—Old English 'Tocketon' and 'Touketon'—was a tiny hamlet which consisted until recently of scattered farms and a few cottages. Until 1872 there were about 60 inhabitants in Tuckton and, as there was no direct access to neighbouring Christchurch until the building of Tuckton Bridge, it remained completely rural until that time.

Besides Tuckton Farm, Elford's Farm and the inevitable smithy there were several large houses in the area. There was Carbery House, owned by F. Moser, a large estate between Pokesdown and Tuckton. A winding drive with dense bushes and magnificent rhododendrons in the spring hid the house from the road. (It has been demolished.) There was farmland all around. Heatherlea, another large estate, was owned by the Hon. Edward William Douglas, J.P. (now demolished) and Stourcliffe House and Farm owned by George Kellaway (also demolished).

For a time in the late 19th century Tuckton achieved fame as the district where Count Tchertkoff and other Russian exiles stayed and printed the works of Tolstoy. (See Chapter Ten.)

## CHAPTER SEVEN

# Services in Bournemouth

## Education

In Bournemouth education was originally provided by voluntary enterprise and two religious societies. The National Society established Church of England schools and the British and Foreign Society established nonconformist schools, both bodies being concerned that many children could not read the Bible.

The need for a church school was recognised by the Rev. Morden Bennett, a great church leader and educationalist, as early as 1846 even though the population was just over

six hundred. The first purpose-built school was opened in 1850 on land adjoining the church—St Peter's School—which satisfied the needs of the area until 1936, when it was demolished and replaced by Maple's furniture stores. By then the centre of the town had changed from being residential and rural to one of mainly business premises.

Objections had been made to the Tractarian and very high-church style of St Peter's Church. In 1868 the foundation stone was laid by Lord Shaftesbury for a church with

94   The Square c.1915, with the Sacred Heart, the previous Punshon Memorial and St Peter's Church in the background.

**95** The Square *c*.1945.

**96** Holy Trinity Church provided the answer for those who wanted a more Evangelistic religion, less High Church than St Peter's. Old Christchurch Road was a quiet, sedate road in those days. The clock on the tower in the centre of the roundabout originally surmounted a nearby tram shelter, which was a gift from Capt. H.B. Norton, J.P. The tram shelter was demolished in 1947.

a simpler and more evangelical style in Old Christchurch Road—Holy Trinity Church. As the congregation reduced as residents moved away from the town centre, the church was sold and in 1973 it was used for medieval banquets. A fire destroyed most of the building and in 1981 it was demolished and replaced by office blocks.

Holy Trinity School was opened in 1869 (which became St Paul's Primary School) and was demolished in 1980). Other National Schools of that period included St Michael's, which was opened in Orchard Street in 1877 and transferred to West Hill Road in 1878, St

of Edmund Haviland-Birke, Liberal M.P. from 1858-74. The older school was then for boys only and a high fence was erected between the two schools, though some of the more daring boys enjoyed peeping through the cracks!

The Education Act of 1870 established board schools in areas where the voluntary system was inadequate. Morden Bennett was firmly opposed to the introduction of board schools in case parents removed their children from church schools; because of his views there was no state education in Bournemouth until the 20th century.

**97** Horse Shoe Common and Holy Trinity Church, 1870.

Clement's, Springbourne in 1880, and St John's, Boscombe, 1893.

Free Church Schools were also founded, the first being the Lansdowne British School in 1858, which opened in a building off Commercial Road, followed by new premises at the corner of Madeira (then Oxford Road). The school closed in 1935 due to lack of numbers and became part of the police station. Other schools included Mrs. Balston's Infant School, Spring Road, Springbourne, 1877-1915 and Boscombe British School, Gladstone Road, 1879, which originally consisted of infants, boys and girls. In 1908 an infants and girls' school was built in adjoining Haviland Road, the name commemorating the services

Until 1877 the few Catholic children in the district were educated at one of the Windsor Cottages, now the site of the Oratory of the Sacred Heart. In 1877 a Catholic school was established at Blenheim House, Lansdowne Road, by Lady Georgiana Fullerton, and two years later it was transferred to Avenue Road. In January 1880 a better site was obtained in Yelverton Road, given through the generosity of Lady Fullerton. It became known as St Walburga's Roman Catholic School (now demolished). From 1929 the school was situated in Malvern Road.

It is not surprising that, due to Bournemouth's balmy climate and health–giving properties, several private schools opened with the aim of providing a more exclusive education than given in the elementary schools. Among them was the Exeter House Collegiate School for Boys (1858-76), the Headmaster of which was Rev. J.H. Wanklyn; it was considered a first-class preparatory school. Later it was sold to H. Newlyn who transformed the house into one of the foremost hotels in the town, first as *Newlyn's Hotel* and today as the *Royal Exeter Hotel*. By 1890 there were 40 private schools; some had a short life but others developed on preparatory and high school lines.

Rivalry developed among some of the private schools as they competed for more pupils. St Margaret's Hall, West Cliff, stressed language and musical instruction, specifying that the school was exclusive to daughters of those in a good social position. Bournemouth Commercial School, established in 1865 in Avenue Road, was 'highly recommended by the resident gentry', while Knole Hall College, Knyveton Road, was a 'refined home where girls are trained to be worthy and self-reliant members of society'.

Cranleigh Ladies' School started in Old Christchurch Road, opposite Holy Trinity Church (now demolished), and in 1883 moved to Bradbourne Road, but shortly after it had to be sold. It was advertised as 'a nice little school in a nice little district near Christchurch'. Fortunately for posterity, it was purchased by Miss Mary Broad and her friend, Miss Thresher, and reopened in 1886, with 30 girls, as Bournemouth High School. Their aim was to provide a first-class liberal education with a good religious basis. By 1888, requiring larger premises, they moved into newly-built Norwich Avenue, near West station, then a little country one.

**98** The staff of Bournemouth High School, 1895, which later became Talbot Heath. Miss Broad is seated in the second row, fourth from the left.

**99** The south front of Bournemouth High School.

After Miss Thresher left, Miss Broad found that the progressive development was too much for one person and handed over the school to a body of governors in trust. In 1935 the continually expanding school moved to its present site among the pine trees of Talbot Woods, changing its name to Talbot Heath School. In 1996 the school celebrated 100 years of growth and educational achievement. Their academic tradition is based on hard work, diligence and the creation of a caring community. Another leading independent school is Wentworth Girls' College.

In 1865 the Private Gentlemen's School was established at Ascham House and Woodcote in Gervis Road. In 1903 the buildings were offered to the town as a central school, but because of strong opposition no action was taken. The need for a municipal high school for girls had been urged for some time. It was not until 1918 that these premises were adapted to become the Bournemouth Girls' School. (For five years previously they had shared accommodation in nearby Bournmouth Municipal College.) The school commenced with 160 pupils and fees as low as from one and a half to three guineas. It was only in 1960 that the school was transferred from the two Victorian houses to its present modern premises, with spacious ground in Castle Lane West.

There was no boys' high school until 1901 when a Municipal Grammar and Technical School was opened in Portchester Road, which in 1939 was transferred to East Way. The former school became Portchester Boys' Secondary School with additional premises in Harewood Avenue. In 1889 there was a science and art school at Poole Hill and also at Drummond Road, Boscombe, where pupil teacher classes were also held, and at Hannington Road, Pokesdown, all replaced by the Municipal College in 1913.

## The Fire Service

There was no fire service in Bournemouth until 1870, although piped-water was available from 1866. Questions had been raised by the Board of Commissioners about obtaining a fire engine. Shortly afterwards a serious fire broke out at Hampstead House on Richmond Hill, the home of Dr. Falls, a prominent doctor and member of the board. Although there were water mains there was no apparatus. A bucket chain from the River Bourne was of little avail and fire engines from Poole and Christchurch arrived too late.

As a result Mr. McWilliam became the first captain of a voluntary fire brigade. He was authorised to purchase a hose and reel costing £67 13s. 6d. and a fireengine at £65. Twenty superintendents were equipped with belts, axes and hose wrenches while 50 labourer firemen operated the manual fire engine. This volunteer fire service of public-spirited men became the forerunner of today's great municipal organisation. Absence or lateness for practices was punishable by a fine of 3d.

Until 1902 appliances were horse drawn and usually employed by job masters, and when a fire occurred the horses could be employed on other work. Eventually two pairs of horses were purchased for fire work only. Problems of communication remained as shown by a telegram received by the Bournemouth Brigade: FIRE AT THROOP STRAW RICK OTHERS NEAR—Hunt, Farmer. The telegram took 20 minutes to arrive!

Fire stations were built, most of which have been replaced by more modern ones.

A feature of the Holdenhurst Road station (now a university students' recreation club) was a beautiful frieze that extended along three sides of the interior depicting fire-fighting from buckets and squirts to the steam fire engine. It has been carefully removed to the modern fire station in Springbourne. The Edwardian fireman's brass pole, the longest in Europe, remains encased in the listed Holdenhurst building, while on its roof is an interesting weather vane of a steam fire engine with horses.

In 1938 the first professional chief officer was appointed when more volunteers were recruited for the auxiliary and emergency fire service. Valiant service was rendered in Bournemouth and other blitzed areas. In 1941 a national fire service was established but after the end of the Second World War county councils and county boroughs were made fire authorities. In a period of about eighty-five years an efficient force had emerged from humble beginnings.

**100** *Below left.* Captain James McWilliam, first Chief of the Bournemouth Volunteer Fire Service, 1870-1877.

**101** *Below right.* Fireman and engineer F.W. White of Boscombe Station saved the lives of these children at a hairdresser's shop at Pokesdown on 30 June 1898.

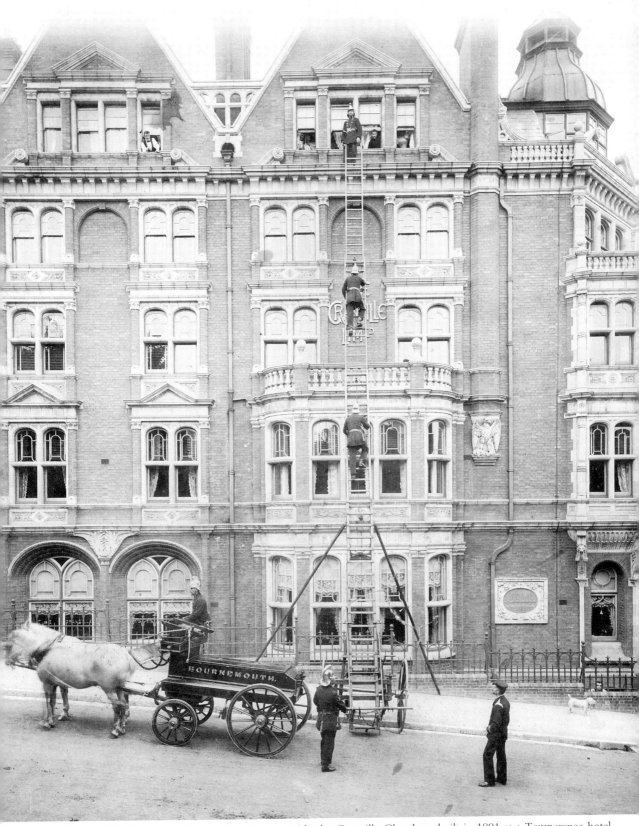

**102** Two horses with firecart and firemen in training outside the Granville Chambers, built in 1891 as a Temperance hotel, and in memory of Dr. A. Granville.

## The Police Force

Hampshire Constabulary was formed in 1839, but Bournemouth which was then a small watering place had no police until 1856. Any police duties required were carried out by the village constabulary from Holdenhurst. From 1856 Bournemouth had one policeman, P.C. Smith, who received from 17s. to 21s. per week, and by 1862 there were two constables and one sergeant who were paid 23s. each weekly.

A police station was built in Oxford Road (now Madeira Road) in 1869 as part of the Ringwood Police Division. Police stations were erected in other parts of Bournemouth while the total police force increased from 14 in 1884 to 44 in 1892. In the following year instructions were given to all members of the Hampshire Constabulary that white linen collars could be worn which had to be kept scrupulously clean. Among the cases dealt with in 1893, the

*Bournemouth Observer* recorded those of Mr. Butterworth who was fined £1 or 10 days' imprisonment for refusing to take his dog off the pier, Luke Holden who was fined £1 for bathing in an unauthorised part of the beach, and Walter Walliken who was given one month's hard labour for sleeping out.

The need for more mobility led to the provision of bicycles for some policemen in about 1896 and seven days' leave was granted to constables and sergeants. More traffic duties resulted from the passing of the Motor Car Act 1903, when speed traps were carried out by means of a stop watch to catch those reckless enough to exceed the speed limit of 20 miles an hour! Until 1919 it was not possible for a single policeman to marry without the permission of the chief constable! As a result of the Second World War women were accepted into the police force and have played an important part since.

**103 & 104**  P.C. Dudman, the first police officer to ride a motorcycle (a Rudge) in Bournemouth during the Second World War and in full uniform, *c.*1940.

**105**   Police outing in 1908—from Boscombe Police Station (since demolished and replaced).

## Transport

The earliest form of public transport in Bournemouth was provided by the Emerald coaches which from 1840 called at Bournemouth twice daily. In about 1850 there were several horse-drawn omnibuses travelling daily between Holmsley (Christchurch) and Hamworthy (Poole), the nearest railway stations.

The first coach service in Bournemouth itself was provided by Henry Laidlow. It was called 'Tally Ho!' and ran between the centre of Bournemouth and its station (opened in 1870).

By the 1880s several horse-drawn omnibuses operated throughout the Bournemouth area. A family business started by Thomas Elliot in 1880 as the Royal Blue Coach Operators was sold in 1936 to the National Express Coach Service. The firm started with a handsome four-in-hand stagecoach. As its popularity increased it owned over 200 horses which were stabled at the Royal Blue Mews in Norwich Avenue. After 1911 the Royal Blue coaches became motorised, but unfortunately in that year Thomas

Elliott was kicked by one of his beloved horses and died. The business was carried on by his sons, Jack, Harry and Ted, who became the youngest four-in-hand drivers licensed to carry passengers. They delivered the first copies of the *Bournemouth Evening* (now *Daily*) *Echo* by pony trap. After the First World War, the two remaining brothers (Ted was killed during the war) continued to develop the business, until in the 1920s it became the largest motorcoach business in the south. A fine coach station was erected by the company in Exeter Road in 1929 which was shared by the Hants and Dorset Motors. Unfortunately it was destroyed by fire in 1976. (Still, 1998, dilapidated.)

Between 1881 and 1899 proposals to construct tramlines between Bournemouth and Poole were opposed by Bournemouth Council on the grounds that the streets were too narrow and that they would spoil their appearance. By 1901 the Poole & District Electric Traction Co. had established a tram route from Poole which had to terminate at the County Gates,

**106**  One of Thomas Elliott's horse-drawn buses.

**107**  Another Royal Blue Stagecoach.

**108**   Edwards' Motor Transport.

**109**   A Bournemouth open-top tram en route from Poole. The top seats were covered with smart cloth, which had to be reversed by the conductor when it rained.

**110**  A serious tram accident occurred in 1908 when the brakes of a tram failed and it crashed into Fairlight Glen in Avenue Road.

Westbourne, the boundary between Bournemouth and Poole. The fare was 3d. Eventually Bournemouth decided it would run its own service within its own borough between Pokesdown and Lansdowne, later extended to other areas in Christchurch, Poole and Bournemouth. Bournemouth then became the first municipality to have tramways in two other towns, the fare being 6d. Everyone was horrified when, in 1908, a serious accident occurred. The brakes of a tram failed and its speed increased to about 70 m.p.h. It became derailed and crashed into the gardens of Fairlight Glen in Avenue Road. Seven passengers were killed and 26 were injured.

Due to strong opposition the tram was not allowed to run on Sundays. In 1910, during the Bournemouth Centenary Festivals, a prize-winning float read: '1810—No Sunday trams. 1910—Still no Sunday trams.' It was not until 1913 that a Sunday afternoon service commenced.

In 1933 an experimental trolley-bus service opened between County Gates and Bournemouth Square. By 1936 it was extended throughout the town. Continual improvements in design have resulted in today's modern buses. The last tram left Christchurch in 1936 carrying the mayors of Christchurch and Bournemouth and other councillors, who then returned on the first trolley-bus. The trams were sold; some were used as garden sheds, caravans and even as dog kennels.

Sailing has always been popular in coastal resorts and the first Bournemouth jetty in 1856 was to provide easier facilities for this. It was a great day in 1871 when the *Heather Bell* sailed from Bournemouth often accompanied by music from the Bournemouth Promenade Band. It was discontinued in 1876 but was succeeded by other vessels, including *Criterion*, *Lord Elgin*, *Windsor Castle* and *Brodick Castle*. At one time competition was so keen that passengers could sail to the Isle of Wight and return for only 4½d.

## Hospitals and Sanatoria

Recognising the advantages of Bournemouth for chest complaints, the governors of Brompton Hospital, London, decided to establish a sanatorium there for consumptive patients with good prospects of a cure.

To obtain money, bazaars and concerts were held at Boscombe Manor and other large houses. The building, costing about £15,000, opened in October 1855, as the National Sanatorium for Consumption and Diseases of the Chest. It was the first sanatorium in this country and the first purpose-built one in the world. It was situated between St Stephen's Road and Bourne Road (then Sanatorium Road) and was surrounded by pine woods. Patients soon came from every county in England. In 1966 the sanatorium became the Royal National Hospital and was closed in 1989 when the new Royal Bournemouth Hospital was opened that year. The building now looks neglected and is boarded up and has been approved for 274 flats for students from Bournemouth University.

Other convalescent homes were built in the 'Invalids' paradise'. The Hahnemann Convalescent Home was opened by Earl Cairns, the Lord Chancellor, on 3 June 1879 for persons of limited means who were in the first stages of consumption. Homeopathic medicines were prescribed and made up on the premises.

The Firs Home, Trinity Road, erected 1868, dealt with advanced cases of consumption; later it became a maternity home but was demolished in 1993. After the break-up of Stourfield Estate in 1893, the house became a private nursing home for consumptive patients. During the First World War it became a sanatorium for servicemen with tuberculosis, and after the war it was used again for civilians. After the Second World War it was taken over by the British T.B. Association and in 1958 became known as Douglas House and part of the hospital service. After almost 100 years of caring for the sick and elderly, patients were transferred to Christchurch Hospital, and in 1989 the building was demolished. Great sadness was felt for the end of an era.

**111** The first purpose-built Consumption Sanatorium in the world, 1855.

**112** Patients enjoying themselves outside the Home Sanatorium, which became Douglas House (now demolished).

Herbert Convalescent Home was built as a memorial to Lord Sidney Herbert of Lee, Secretary of War, 1852-55, who died in 1861 at Wilton House. In 1874 a convalescent home was established at Blenheim House, Lansdowne Road, by Lady Georgiana Fullerton, a well-known writer of that period and a kind philanthropist. After her death in 1885, it seemed that the home might have to close. Rescue came from the Sisters of Mercy in London who rented premises in Branksome Wood Road, which became St Joseph's Convalescent Home. The Convalescent Home cared for many patients until 1992 when it opened as a Sanctuary for H.I.V. and Aids sufferers. The home closed in 1996 through lack of funds.

Until the middle of the 19th century the government did not consider the health of the nation was its concern, despite outbreaks of cholera. There were no free facilities in Bournemouth for the treatment of the poor who had to travel to dispensaries at Southampton or Dorchester.

Charles Packe, a member of the Board of Commissioners, became concerned about the welfare of the community and arranged a meeting with doctors and other prominent citizens. As a result on 15 October 1859 a public dispensary was established at 2 Grenville Cottages, Yelverton Road, to provide free medical service to the poor of Bournemouth and for those with incomes under one pound a week. A move to Madeira Vale in 1868 was made when larger premises were required. Land was provided by Mr. Kerley for £200. The need arose for a cottage hospital for infectious diseases, but this met with opposition. The building was completed in 1876 and was purchased by the Boscombe Dispensary Committee for the Boscombe, Pokesdown and Springbourne Infirmary, with 12 beds for local artisans who paid a small weekly sum for treatment—the beginning of the real hospital service.

Larger premises were again required and in 1898 a much bigger hospital with many additional wards was constructed in Ashley Road, Boscombe. There was still a shortage of accommodation, and by 1909 new extensions were opened by Princess Alexandra.

As the Golden Jubilee of Queen Victoria approached, it was suggested that a new hospital was built for those living in West Bournemouth. Land was given by Clapcott Dean and on 21 June 1887 the foundation stone was laid by E.W. Rebbeck, Chairman of the Commissioners. With permission from the queen, it was named the Royal Victoria Hospital.

In 1912 the two hospitals were amalgamated under the title of the Royal Victoria and West Hants Hospital, resulting in a further period of growth and more specialisation.

When the ultra-modern Royal Bournemouth Hospital was opened in December 1989, based on the latest technology, the older hospitals, which had given excellent service, had deteriorated greatly. Boscombe Hospital was demolished in 1992 and replaced by a housing estate. The Royal Victoria Hospital, with its fine reputation as one of the best eye hospitals in the country, is planned to close by 1999 and will be rehoused in modern, new buildings in the Royal Bournemouth Hospital.

**113** Royal Victoria and West Hants. Hospital, Boscombe which was demolished in 1992.

**114** The main entrance to the Royal Bournemouth Hospital, a modern hospital in an attractive setting. A wide range of services is provided to patients in Bournemouth, Christchurch and beyond.

**115**  Elizabeth Collins, whose dancing qualifications were delayed because of the typhoid epidemic.

## Typhoid Epidemic

In late summer 1936 there was a serious typhoid epidemic in Bournemouth, Poole and Christchurch which claimed 718 victims and resulted in 70 deaths.

Elizabeth Collins, then aged 18, was training to become a teacher of ballet, and was staying in a farm in a little village in Shropshire; she became unwell for, seemingly, no reason whatever. A mysterious illness had been affecting people in Bournemouth, and people, in increasing numbers, had visited their doctors to complain of gastric disorders. Most doctors in the area had never come across a case of typhoid. One of the first G.P.s to recognise it was Dr. J.H. Bentley who was called in by a colleague to see a sick patient with the characteristic, erratic, high and low temperature. Dr. Vernon Shaw, a great epidemiologist, discovered that contaminated milk from Frowd's Dairy was a main factor. It had been supplied by the newly opened, very modern farm. The milk had been drunk by many unsuspecting people. A nearby stream from which cows had drunk had become contaminated after a sewage tank had overflowed. It was also discovered that there was a carrier, local M.P. Captain Hambro of Merley House, who was shocked to hear that he was the typhoid carrier and that a sewage tank there had overflowed and spread the disease. Pasteurised milk was then introduced in Bournemouth, the first town to receive it.

Among the epidemic victims was Dennis Long, the 10-year-old son of the dairy owners who were forced into receivership. Among other survivors were a former Poole mayor, Peter Coles, Edna Travis, a former 'Mother Christmas', her mother, twin brothers and cousin. Edna was the last victim, then 11 years old. Her father, a chauffeur, was away in London, and no one realised that the children were alone in the house in Windham Road, where they lived on stale bread and Oxo, all they had. The house had a large yellow cross put on it. When Edna' later caught the disease, she vowed that if her family survived she would become a fever nurse. When she reached 17 she kept her word.

Sixty years later a strange reunion took place at Merley House, when 14 of the survivors, including Elizabeth Collins, met, after reading of the suggestion from the survivor, Dennis Long.

The epidemic made medical history.

## CHAPTER EIGHT

# The Bournemouth Symphony Orchestra

During the 19th century Bournemouth was described as a 'paradise of pines for wealthy invalids', elegant, genteel, but stuffy and dull. That the invalid resort emerged with a musical reputation which spread throughout the world is little more than miraculous.

The miracle was due to the appointment in 1893 of Dan Godfrey Jnr., the son of a famous Grenadier Guards bandmaster, and the fact that he stayed in Bournemouth in spite of much unjust criticism from the council. His short-term contract of £95 per week (out of which he was to play three times daily from Whitsuntide to October, supply uniforms, music and pay his 30 musicians), was criticised,

as there was already a small, military Italian band playing on the pier led by Signor Bertini. It was paid for by public subscription, and in 1892 it became the nucleus of the first Corporation Military Band.

On opening night in the Winter Gardens, a large, glass dome-like structure, built in 1876, the new orchestra played to an audience of 5,000 among palms and pot plants. In October, nearing the end of Godfrey's contract, his famous father, Lieutenant Dan Godfrey, brought his Grenadier band to Bournemouth when his band played together with the orchestra of about 70 musicians. Its outstanding success persuaded the council, to renew

MR. DAN GODFREY.

**116**   Dan Godfrey and the Bournemouth Municipal Orchestra (later Bournemouth Symphony Orchestra).

**117**    The magnificent glass structure of the old Winter Gardens, with its exotic plants, was opened in 1877.

Godfrey's contract for the winter months. For this period 25 double-handed musicians played in the Winter Gardens and on the pier.

In 1895 Godfrey made his first move towards symphony music by announcing that classical music would be given each Thursday, soon extended to Mondays and Thursdays. Admission was one shilling. By 1896 Godfrey received a permanent appointment as musical director and general manager of the Winter Gardens. There were more arguments about the three-year contract at £700 per annum. The council would take over the orchestra which became the first Municipal Orchestra in Britain.

Godfrey's aim was to increase the strength of his orchestra and encourage good music and particularly British music. Every seat was taken when Adelina Patti sang and, again, in 1897, when the famous conductor, Sir August Manns, directed symphonies by Schumann and Schubert. A letter of praise from the distinguished conductor also pointed out that the

orchestra needed to be strengthened. Godfrey made the letter public and received more instrumentalists.

Besides arranging popular and classical music, he was also expected to stage variety shows, with dancers, comedians and even jugglers, but wherever possible he would insert parts of a symphony. By 1900 despite continuing arguments about the cost of the orchestra, he was able to introduce chamber music to the town.

Many famous musicians came to the old Winter Gardens and conducted their own work, including Stanford, Coleridge-Taylor, Elgar, Holst, who once cycled 110 miles from London to Bournemouth, and Hubert Parry who was born in Bournemouth. Bournemouth's first anniversary was celebrated in 1910 with a great concert when many British composers shared the platform with Godfrey and in 1911 he persuaded the council to create a separate military band for the pier, relieving the orchestra of this duty.

During the First World War, although some members were called up and there were smaller audiences due to the blackout, the orchestra continued to play patriotic music, British music and the music of our allies. After the war attendances remained low and the council considered reducing the number of players and even scrapping the orchestra altogether. Reluctantly Godfrey agreed to the disbandment of the military band and that his orchestra of 41 players would play on the pier again in addition to the Winter Gardens.

Supporters were horrified to hear of the financial plight of the Municipal Orchestra, particularly Dame Ethel Smythe, whose work had been played by Godfrey when other orchestras would not accept music from a woman composer. To show her gratitude, she suggested to important colleagues that a knighthood should be bestowed on Godfrey. On 3 June 1922, his birthday, he was knighted in recognition of his valuable services to British music. That night a delighted orchestra played 'For he's a jolly good fellow', while the council, impressed by his popularity, realised that it could not decimate this amazing orchestra.

However the Winter Gardens had become an anacronism in the growing modern town.

**118** In 1934 Richard Austin became the conductor. When the orchestra was reduced and hours and salaries were considerably shortened, he resigned.

A new pavilion was proposed. The *Belle Vue Hotel* and Assembly Rooms were demolished and a splendid edifice, with bright colours, was erected, opened by the Duke of Gloucester on 19 March 1929. To the disappointment of Sir Dan the orchestra had only a minor part to play. In September 1934 he retired. The 'Glass House', the 'Cucumber Frame', names given to the Winter Gardens—remained deserted. Before its demolition, Sir Dan conducted the orchestra for the last time. The hall was crowded as the rain beat on the glass roof while the orchestra played Haydn's 'Farewell Symphony'. Each player extinguished a candle and left the platform. The final one was snuffed out by Sir Dan and darkness reigned. A month later the building was a shell.

In 1934 Richard Austin was appointed as conductor. To increase attendance he reorganised the orchestra so that some of the 46 musicians would play outdoors and others indoors for orchestral concerts. Performances were increased and many more concerts were given. When the Second World War started attendances again became poor. The orchestra was reduced to 24; hours were shortened and salaries were reduced to £4 a week. Austin promptly resigned.

An independent body of redundant musicians and supporters began to play symphonies on Monday lunch-times and evenings to war workers. The remainder of the Municipal Orchestra played popular Sunday evening concerts under Monty Birch, a long-time member of Godfrey's orchestra. The presence of evacuees, government departments, and servicemen stationed in Bournemouth meant that both concerts were well supported.

After the war, a new red-brick concert hall, with ideal acoustics, was constructed. Rudolf Schwarz, an Austrian, was appointed as musical director. After some early criticism he became a great success. After war-weary years a new and enthusiastic audience had emerged. Schwarz resigned in 1950 to become musical director of the Birmingham Symphony Orchestra. He was succeeded by Charles Groves of the BBC Northern Orchestra. Soon there was a strike and other problems and Groves found himself playing to half-empty concerts, followed by threats of closure or a reduced orchestra. In 1952 the council decided to disband the orchestra. Fortunately, Sir John Barbirolli conducted the Hallé Orchestra the following night. In a speech to a crowded audience he informed them that there would have been a revolution in Manchester if the council had attempted to take his orchestra away from him. 'You must support your orchestra to the hilt and show your council that you cannot do without it.' Because of publicity and an appeal fund set up by a Winter Gardens Society, the council reversed its decision, but expected the orchestra to play in the Pavilion ballroom in the mornings, the bandstand in the afternoon and symphonies in the evenings.

Diminished audiences continued, and in 1953 notice was given to the orchestra; after 62 years of chequered history the Municipal Orchestra came to an end. The Winter Gardens Society, with support from arts councils, acted swiftly. They would be responsible for costs. A regional orchestra was established that would visit areas in the west of England. The orchestra would be in the hands of a new body, the Western Orchestral Society Ltd., and the name would be changed to Bournemouth Symphony Orchestra.

After Groves' resignation during a period of ten years' hard work, a famous Rumanian conductor, Constantin Silvestri, was appointed, whose glamour and international fame produced packed houses again. The dazzling period ended with his death at the age of fifty-five. He had requested that he be buried near the Winter Gardens and the sea which he loved so much. His grave is close to that of Sir Dan Godfrey who died in July 1939.

Although financial problems occurred again, these were overcome by the support of the Friends of the Bournemouth Orchestras and better support from local authorities.

## CHAPTER NINE

# War Years

The serenity of Bournemouth was hardly disturbed during the First World War but this cannot be said of the Second World War.

Bournemouth became a reception area for evacuees from Southampton, Portsmouth and London, and many vital offices were trans-ferred to the town and established in some of the large hotels. Troops, including Americans and Canadians, were accommodated in others. Soon refugees from Nazi oppression arrived—German Jews, Austrians, Czechoslovakians and Poles.

In the *Royal Bath Hotel* there were Canadians, R.A.F. and other officers. American soldiers were lodged at the *Palace Court* and *Ambassadors* hotels and American Red Cross at the *Marsham Court Hotel*. Troops were billeted in the College of Technology and in Wentworth Mount Girls School (now Wentworth College), the girls having been evacuated to Wales. After the evacuation of Dunkirk in 1940 French soldiers appeared for the first time, dirty 'scruffs' showing signs of the suffering they had undergone. Later the 'Desert Rats' came, tired and dishevelled, before leaving for D-Day.

An Area Defence Ban was soon in force and few civilian visitors were allowed into the town. The seafront was closed to all but the

**119** French and Belgian troops in Wimborne Road, Moor-down, after the evacuation of Dunkirk, *c.*1940.

military, the beach bristled with barbed wire and army vehicles were stationed along the clifftops. Gaps were cut in Bournemouth and Boscombe piers. On Hengistbury Head there were tanks, tank trenches and miles of barbed wire.

Despite the inky black-out, cinemas were crowded with soldiers and civilians. Weekly dances were given by the Americans, socials were held by church organisations, and concerts continued at the Pavilion. Cinema programmes were changed several times weekly, and entry was charged at 6d., 9d., and 1s. If the audience was caught by air-raid warnings, impromptu music was played and if public transport was suspended people walked home.

Rationing of bacon, ham, butter and sugar started in 1940, followed by meat, tea and cooking fats, cheese and sweets. Clothes rationing started in June 1941, and 66 coupons had to last for a year, which was cut to 51 the following year. Shortages and rationing meant that people had little on which to spend their money.

Although Bournemouth escaped the devastation that many of the major industrial towns experienced, it did not escape bomb damage and suffering. The town was raided about 50 times; 219 persons were killed, 75 premises were destroyed. In all, over 2,000 bombs were dropped. The first air-raid took place on 3 June 1940 when a house in Cellar Farm Road. Southbourne was destroyed and 19 other properties nearby were damaged. In September 1940 there was a direct hit on the orphanage wing of the House of Bethany. Fortunately the children had been placed elsewhere, but the convent and also several nearby houses were damaged.

One of the worst raids occurred in November 1940 when 53 people were killed and 2,321 properties were damaged. Parts of Westbourne, including Christ Church suffered £1,000-worth of damage. Malmesbury Park area and Alma Road, Winton, were badly devastated and Alma Road Elementary School, which had opened in 1908, received a direct hit and became a maze of torn and twisted masonry. Skerryvore, formerly the home of Robert Louis Stevenson, was destroyed by a bomb. Soldiers stationed at Skerryvore and people living in the adjoining Robert Louis Stevenson Avenue were killed.

**120**  Alma Road School, badly bomb damaged, 1940.

**121 & 122**  *Above and below left.* Skerryvore, Robert Louis Stevenson's house from 1884–87, and after bomb damage in November 1940.

**123**  *Below right.* The *Metropole Hotel* was also destroyed by bombs.

On 23 May 1943 more serious damage was caused when bombs were dropped on 10 districts; the *Central Hotel* in Richmond Hill and *Metropole Hotel* were practically destroyed. Canadian, American and Australian soldiers, who were stationed in the latter hotel, were killed. Beale's department store was completely burnt out after a direct hit from an H.E. bomb,

**124** The Drill Hall, Lansdowne Road, Bournemouth, was occupied by the Home Guard during the war years. In 1947 it was again occupied by the Territorial Army and in the same year the unit received the A.A. Gun, assembled it, and were being given further instructions. R.S.M. Lawrence and his wife Kathleen had the flat above the Drill Hall as their married quarters.

followed by an explosion of its gas main. Allen's, now part of Dingle's, was badly affected by the destruction of Beale's, as the wind blew flames in its direction. West's cinema, on the site of the Burlington Arcade, originally known as Shaftesbury Hall commemorating Lord Shaftesbury's work for the poor, received a direct hit. The Punshon Church, which was then in Richmond Hill, was extensively damaged. Many other churches, houses and bus premises were partially destroyed: there were 77 dead and over 3,000 buildings seriously scarred.

After the raids thousands of enquiries were dealt with at the administrative centre in the Town Hall, including problems of rationing, billeting, damage to property and removal of furniture and stores. Help was given from the Assistance Board, WRVS, CAB, Soldiers, Sailors and Air Force Association and others. Rest centres were opened. In the local *Echo* letters of gratitude were printed about the services of the Police, NFS, Civil Defence, WRVS and others.

After the war Bournemouth had been left shabby and scarred; there were ruined and unpainted buildings, loose scaffolding, a short-age of houses, derelict piers and the rusty remains of defence weapons littered along the shoreline and in the sea. The beach, due to the strong winds and heavy tides had become a narrow strip of sand. The daunting task of restoring the town to its former beauty lay ahead.

## CHAPTER TEN

# The People of Bournemouth

## Early Pioneers

**Merton** and **Annie Russell-Cotes**. Sir Merton Russell-Cotes, an outstanding pioneer of Bournemouth, had many progressive ideas and was a benefactor to the town. He was born in 1835 in Staffordshire and from childhood was enamoured with pictures, *objets d'art* and antiques. When he was 18 it was discovered he had congestion of the right lung, and on

medical advice he spent time in South America and other foreign places for the benefit of his health; he always added to his growing collection. After his period as manager of the *Royal Hanover Hotel*, Glasgow, recurring attacks of bronchitis resulted in visits to the south coast, including Bourne where he and his wife stayed at the *Bath Hotel*. There he met the owner who wished to sell the hotel, and persuaded

**125 & 126** Merton and Annie Russell-Cotes became Honorary Freemen in 1908. A knighthood was bestowed on Merton the following year.

Russell-Cotes to purchase it with the result that he took possession of it on Christmas Day 1876. The Duke of Argyll, who was staying at the hotel, advised Russell-Cotes to enlarge and improve it, as he considered that it could become the most distinguished hotel in the town. With the addition of the prefix *Royal* it was re-opened in August 1880.

Soon the hotel was resplendent with priceless paintings by Turner, Corot, Edwin Long, Landseer and exquisite Japanese and Chinese curios and it was soon described as a temple of luxury and of art.

The *Royal Bath* soon boasted many royal visitors, such as the Empress Eugenie, the Queen of Sweden, the King of the Belgians, and Edward VII when he was a young Prince of Wales. By 1883 Russell-Cotes was elected to the Board of Commissioners. He had many ideas for the improvement of Bournemouth, including an Undercliff Drive for the benefit of invalids and to prevent erosion. To over-come criticisms of dullness he suggested a

pavilion near the pier entrance. He also spent time working for a fever hospital when he was supported by several doctors in the area. But the idea of a fever hospital horrified many residents, and to his distress his effigy, with those of some of the commissioners, was burnt. Through worry and strain he became ill again and went abroad. On his return the hospital had been built and given the name of 'sanitary', which had been suggested by his wife. It is now part of the Royal Victoria Hospital in Gloucester Road.

When in 1890 Bournemouth became a Municipal Borough, the following year, to show their pleasure and to enhance the dignity of the town, Russell-Cotes and his wife presented a mace and mayoral badge, with an 18-carat loop, enamelled with the Hampshire rose. The motto *Pulchritudo et Salubritas*, engraved on the badge, would make known the health and beauty of the little town. In the same year he was invited to become mayor but refused until the council accepted his suggestion,

**127** Undercliff Drive. The first section of the Undercliff Drive was commenced in 1907, after many arguments. The pier and the Purbecks can be seen in the distance.

**128** Russell-Cotes Art Gallery and Museum, formerly East Cliff Hall.

in 1894, for an Undercliff Drive, and on their condition that he also became a magistrate.

To celebrate the event and as a birthday present for Annie, the magnificent East Cliff Hall (now the Russell-Cotes Art Gallery and Museum) was built. Besides being their home it would house the increasing treasures brought from abroad.

After further delays the first section of the Undercliff Drive between the pier and Meyrick Road was commenced in 1907. Tributes were showered on Russell-Cotes. He demonstrated appreciation of this great achievement by donating his collection of treasures to his beloved town, while his wife presented their home as an art gallery and museum with a fund for their maintenance. For their generosity and unceasing work they were both made Honorary Freemen of the Borough in 1908.

The following year King Edward VII bestowed a knighthood on Merton. On their Diamond Wedding Anniversary in 1920, they donated many more gifts to the town.

Lady Russell-Cotes died in April 1920 and her husband in the following January. Both were greatly mourned and were buried in an elaborate mausoleum at Rush Corner (now Cemetery Junction).

The art gallery and museum in their elegant home displays a fine collection of Victorian treasures, about three-fifths from Sir Merton's own collection and the remainder were donated after his death. Lady Russell-Cotes' drawing room and boudoir (where she died) retain the charming atmosphere of Victorian prosperity and their love of acquiring beautiful and unusual objects.

**John Elmes Beale** was a contemporary of Merton Russell-Cotes, and actively connected with the development of Bournemouth and was a strong advocate of the need for an Undercliff Drive. In 1906 he became the first local Freeman of the Borough. Appreciation of his work on the council, including three years as mayor and magistrate, was shown by the presentation of a fine portrait of him in mayoral robes which hangs in the mayor's parlour. Two other paintings of Mr. and Mrs. Beale, displayed in Beale's stores, were presented in recognition of their services.

John Elmes Beale was born in Weymouth on 6 December 1847. After business training in Manchester he was employed as assistant in a draper's shop in Weymouth. During this period he became an active member of the Wesleyan church and a local circuit preacher in nearby villages. Looking for a new opening in the surrounding area, he purchased a small shop in Bournemouth at 3 St Peter's Terrace (now part of Hinton Road), where the Fancy Fair was started, selling buckets, spades, boats and toys for a few pence each. From these small beginnings came the present fashionable department stores. Five-shilling train excursions from London and elsewhere soon attracted large crowds. For a time Mr. Beale became a partner in a draper's shop in Commercial Road, opened in 1889 by W.H. Okey, who sold out the following year. The shop then became known as Bealesons' (now discontinued).

The First World War slowed down business, but soon new departments were developed. During the Second World War it was severely bombed, but undeterred it rose from the ashes and prospered.

For many years J. Elmes Beale was a church officer at Richmond Hill United Reformed Church and became deacon in 1896. In l905 J. Bennett Beale joined his father as a deacon and in 1937 he, too, was chosen as mayor. A tradition of service has been established by successive members of the Beale family.

**129 & 130**  John Elmes Beale and Mrs. Beale (the original portraits are in Beale's Department Store).

**131** Beale's Fancy Fair founded in 1881.

**132** In partnership with Okeys. Deliveries by their early-type van.

Frank Beale has been a mayor, a councillor and an elder of the Church for many years and his aunt, Mrs. Rita Beale, became one of the first lady elders. Beale's fashion store has remained a mostly independent and family-owned concern, and Nigel Beale, the great-grandson of the founder, is the current chairman of the store.

**William E. Rebbeck** of Cranborne (1803-1879) came to Bourne as bailiff to the Tregonwell Estate. In 1845 he started his own business, while continuing to manage the Tregonwell estate. He leased from Sir George Gervis a triangular plot of land at the corner of Gervis and Old Christchurch Road on which he built a small, picturesque office. It became known as Rebbecks' Corner, as it was occupied by several members of the Rebbeck family. The premises were demolished in May 1935 when Rebbecks' moved to their present offices in Exeter Road.

As Rebbecks' were the only estate agents for many years, they were concerned with the sale of many large estates including parts of Boscombe Manor, Moordown and Kinson estates, and Chewton Joy Estate (now Chewton Glen). After the sale of the Branksome Tower's Estate in 1892, Rebbecks' acquired the historic

**133**  The second office of Fox & Son in Holdenhurst Road, 1892-1961.

entrance lodge as their Westbourne branch, which remained their office for over 80 years until it was demolished for road widening and office blocks. Many people were dismayed by its disappearance as it had marked the boundary between Bournemouth and Poole, standing among acres of pine forests. The Rebbeck family also had a history of service to the town. Both W.E. Rebbeck and his son, E. Wise Rebbeck, became chairmen of the Board of Commissioners and in 1891 his son became the second mayor. The last member of the family to be associated with the firm, Colonel T.V. Rebbeck, was also a member of the council for many years and mayor from 1936 to 1937.

His death in 1942 marked the last family link with the firm, but the name 'Rebbeck' lives on and their 150th anniversary was celebrated in 1995.

**Anthony Stoddart Fox**, born in London in 1838, came to Bournemouth in 1889 and opened an office in Holdenhurst Road which he shared with a coach builder. As his sons joined the business they moved to larger premises in Holdenhurst Road, over which the family lived. The premises were closed in 1961 and the staff were transferred to Old Christchurch Road.

During the 19th century the firm was concerned with the sale of various estates, including Boscombe Manor to R. Sobey, parts of the Portman, Cooper-Dean estates and also land at Iford and Littledown. As the firm grew, they acquired several smaller businesses, including that of Hankinson, the second estate agent to open in Bournemouth.

**The Mooring Aldridge family** of Christchurch were also connected with the early days of Bournemouth. Matthew Aldridge was mentioned in the Christchurch Award of 1805 and Henry Mooring Aldridge had an office in Poole and then opened one in Bournemouth, c.1860; he purchased one of the first villas in Westover Road. An office was built in the rear part of the plot, known as Hinton Chambers, Hinton Road. Later he built a family home, which was named 'Westover' in Portarlington Road. He had six sons and four daughters. Four of the sons became solicitors. Hewit, the elder son, practised on his own, and later with his son, Kenneth. Harold and Erkinwald worked in their father's practice and were joined by John Haydon, Clerk of the Peace. The fourth son, Gerald A. Mooring Aldridge, served in the First World War. When he left the army in 1919 the family helped him to set up on his own in Winton, where he was joined by A.H. Brownlee, first as an articled clerk and then as a partner, when a further office was opened at the Lansdowne. The name became Aldridge & Brownlee, while Mooring Aldridge & Haydon's amalgamation with another firm of solicitors resulted in the name Lester Aldridge, with branches in many parts of the Bournemouth area.

The name Mooring Aldridge is still well known and respected in Bournemouth whilst members of the family remain connected with the town's oldest firm of solicitors.

**James Druitt Snr.** (1816-1904) was the founder of J & W.H. Druitt, solicitors, Bournemouth, with which the family was connected until 1945 when their interests were sold. James Druitt was a councillor and mayor of Christchurch five times between 1850 and 1896. He became the third clerk to the Board of Commissioners from 1861-77 when he was succeeded by his son, James Druitt Jnr., who held the post until 1890. When Bournemouth attained Municipal-Borough status in 1890 the father was appointed the first town clerk, thus ensuring continuity of service. His son also served as a councillor and became mayor in 1914.

The family's former home is the present Christchurch Library, which was donated to the council together with Druitt Gardens in *c.*1950.

**Robert Day** (1822-1873) was Bournemouth's first photographer. His studio-hut adjoined the Scotch Church (St Andrew's Presbyterian) which used to be at the foot of Richmond Hill. Many of his excellent photographs were purchased by Bournemouth Library, Lansdowne from his son, W.J. Day, who continued in the business after his father's death.

Another close friend of W.J.'s was the Chinese giant, Chang Woo Gow, who retired to Bournemouth in 1890 to obtain relief from suspected tuberculosis. He had appeared in stage shows throughout the world and even been fêted by royalty. He died of a broken heart in November 1893 shortly after the death of his dear wife. He was described by William Day as one of the kindest and gentlest persons he had ever known.

**134** Robert Day, the first professional photographer in Bournemouth, gets ready to take a photograph.

**135**  After the death of Robert Day in 1873, his widow, Emily Day, started the firm of E. Day & Son, William being only 18 years of age and a minor.

**136**  Chang Woo Gow, the Chinese Giant, who came to Bournemouth to improve his health. Here he is seen with Mabel Day, daughter of William Day, his close friend, who was with him when he died.

## The Shelley Connection

Although Bournemouth lacks the background of its two distinguished neighbours, many literary and eminent people have been attracted to the area during the 190 years of its existence.

Of all such literary figures, the Shelley family has had the longest connection. Sir Percy Florence Shelley was the only surviving child of Percy Bysshe Shelley, who was tragically drowned in the Gulf of Spezia in July 1822, and of Mary Wollstonecraft Shelley, the author of *Frankenstein* and other works. He was born in Florence on 12 November 1819 and succeeded to the title on the death in 1844 of his grandfather, Sir Timothy Shelley, inheriting the family estate at Field Place, Horsham, West Sussex. By that time the building had deteriorated. Neither his famous mother nor his wife, Jane, the widow of the Hon. Charles Robert St John, wanted to live there.

In 1849 Sir Percy bought land in the undeveloped area of Boscombe, hoping that the balmy climate and health-giving pines would benefit both his wife and his mother. Land in Boscombe was cheap and was separated from Bournemouth by dense woods and heathland. The only building in the area was a small cottage, known as Boscombe Cottage,[1] standing in 17 acres of ground. From *c.*1801 it was occupied by Philip Norris. After the Inclosure Act of 1802 the estate was increased to over 150 acres. Other occupiers included Richard Norris (1807-11), Robert Heathcote (1811-16), after whom Heathcote Road, Boscombe, is named, James Dover (1819-40) and Major Stephenson, who was the last person to live there before Sir Percy.

Boscombe Cottage has had many changes of name, including Boscombe Alcove[2] and Boscombe House. When it was purchased by

Sir Percy it was known as Boscombe Lodge, but the name was altered to Boscombe Place,[3] probably after the Field Place Estate. In 1873 it was further enlarged and given the more imposing title of Boscombe Manor.

Unfortunately Mary Shelley never lived in Boscombe Manor. She died at her London Home in Chester Square on 1 February 1851. Sir Percy lived at Boscombe Manor until his death in 1849 and Lady Shelley until her death 10 years later. During that time the house became famous as a centre of culture, literature and drama. On the estate Sir Percy lived the life of a wealthy, country gentleman. His many guests included Robert Louis Stevenson, Sir Henry Drummond Wolff, Sir Henry Irving, and friends of Mary Shelley, such as Trelawny, Leigh Hunt, Jefferson Hogg and Shelley's sisters. In Boscombe Manor there was a specially constructed theatre, built in 1866, which replaced a temporary one in the garden. It seated about 200 people, with a gallery and private box from which Lady Shelley could view the performance. It had a large stage and drop-scene of Lerici, Italy, the last home of Percy Bysshe Shelley, painted by his son. Some plays were written by Sir Percy and both he and his wife performed in them. In a place of honour stood a bust of Sir Henry Irving, presented by the actor to Lady Shelley.

In a recess in Lady Shelley's boudoir was the Sanctum, a room kept sacred to the memory of Percy Bysshe and Mary Shelley. The room contained Shelley manuscripts, a miniature by Duc de Montpensier of Shelley holding a book of Sophocles, which, together with a book of Keats, was discovered in his coat pockets after he was drowned. In a glass case were locks of hair of friends, such as Lord Byron, Leigh Hunt, Edward Williams (who was drowned with Shelley), Trelawny, two of Mary's children and of Mary herself. Over the mantelpiece was a portrait of Mary Shelley; the ceiling was painted with stars under which, it is said, visiting children talked in whispers because of the relics of the dead.

In a niche stood a life-size model of a monument by the sculptor, Henry Weekes, commissioned by Sir Percy in memory of his parents. The original in white marble can be seen in Christchurch Priory where it was placed after being rejected by the Rev. Morden Bennett because it could make his church a showplace.

A Shelley legend was gradually created by Lady Jane who gradually edited many of the poet's works and letters, and removed from them many passages she considered unfavourable. A cult of Shelley worshippers was eventually established. After consideration, Sir Percy and Lady Shelley decided that Thomas Jefferson Hogg, a friend of Shelley since his schooldays, would be the most suitable person to undertake a biography of the poet. When they read the first two of the four proposed volumes, they were horrified by what they read which they considered a fantastic caricature of the poet and immediately withdrew all their material from Hogg. In the following year Lady Shelley

**137** Percy Bysshe Shelley, tragically drowned in the Gulf of Spezia in 1822.

**138** The original part of Boscombe Manor, the home for many years of Sir Percy Florence and Lady Jane Shelley.

**139** The proscenium arch of the Shelley Theatre, the first theatre in Bournemouth.

brought out her own *Shelley Memorial* containing selected letters and biographical notes. She destroyed documents which she considered unsuitable for publication and unfavourable to Shelley and also acquired material of which she approved. In 1882 she published four volumes entitled *Shelley and Mary*, containing letters and documents which she considered would be of use for a future history of Shelley.

In 1886, 64 years after Shelley's death, an approved biography was published by Edward Dowden, professor of English literature in the University of Dublin, which remained the standard work for many years.

In a large family vault in St Peter's churchyard the following members of the family are buried: Mary Wollstonecraft Shelley, d.1851,

the second wife of the poet and mother of Percy Florence Shelley. Her body was brought from Chester Place, London, where she died. William Godwin, d.1836, a radical freethinker, and Mary Wollstonecraft Godwin, d.1797, author of *Vindication of the Rights of Women*, the parents of Mary Wollstonecraft Shelley, were originally buried in St Pancras Cemetery. After a Parliamentary Bill authorised the building of a railway through the churchyard their bodies were brought to Bournemouth to be laid beside their daughter. Sir Percy Shelley, d.1889 and Lady Jane Shelley d. 1899, also rest in the family vault.

The heart of Percy Bysshe Shelley, snatched from the burning funeral pyre in Italy by Captain Trelawny, was kept at Boscombe Manor until the death of Sir Percy, when it is said to have been buried with him in the literary shrine in St Peter's churchyard. After Lady Shelley's death in 1899 Boscombe Manor was inherited by the 5th Baron Abinger, a descendant of the Shelley family. Since then it has been owned by various people and in 1937 was purchased by Bournemouth Corporation for £37,000. During the Second World War it became an A.R.P. Centre and at present it is occupied by the Department of Foundation Studies of Bournemouth and Poole College of Art and Design.

When the Casa Magni Museum at Lerici had to be sold for financial reasons, the collected works were donated in 1979 by Margaret Brown, MBE, the founder and curator of the original Italian museum, to the Bournemouth Borough Council, to be housed in two rooms at Boscombe Manor, the home of the poet's son for 40 years. Here students of the works of Shelley can come and browse in the reference library and admire the portraits and mementoes kept in the museum.

**140** The white marble statue in memory of Percy Bysshe and Mary Shelley in Christchurch Priory, after being rejected by the vicar of St Peter's Church, Bournemouth.

**141** Cliff Cottage, *c*.1810, where Charles Darwin stayed from 31 August 1862 to the end of September (now demolished).

**Charles Darwin** spent one month in Bournemouth in September 1862 when one of his sons caught scarlet fever; later his wife also caught it. He rented Cliff Cottage, a thatched cottage built in *c*.1810 and situated in several acres of wooded ground. It was demolished in *c*.1876 when various apartment houses were erected on the site. Darwen found the area uninteresting and wrote to his botanical friend, J.D. Hooker,

> This is a nice but barren country and I can find nothing to look at. Even the brooks and ponds produce nothing. The country is like Patagonia. My wife is almost well, thank God, and soon home.

He was more than delighted when they were able to return home to Downe House, Downe, Kent, at the end of September.

**Paul Verlaine**, born at Metz in France in 1844, enjoyed in Bournemouth one of the few happy periods of his life, most of which was ruined by alcoholism and dissipation. Verlaine came to England in 1876 after serving a prison sentence in Belgium for wounding his former friend, Rimbaud. After teaching for a short time in Lincolnshire, he came to Bournemouth where he was appointed tutor to the Rev. Frederick Remington's private school, St Aloysius. Later the school became part of the *Sandbourne Hotel* in Poole Road. In March 1877 it moved to a larger house, renamed the Villa Remington (now flats). Verlaine left Bournemouth in September 1877 after finding peace and comfort at the newly consecrated Oratory of the Sacred Heart in Richmond Hill. During his stay he wrote two poems about Bournemouth, describing its calm and beauty, 'La mer de Bournemouth' and 'Bournemouth'. On leaving Bournemouth he returned to Paris where he succumbed again to a life of debauchery and died in poverty in 1896.

**Emilie Charlotte Breton** was born in Jersey in October 1853, and became one of London's most celebrated society ladies under her married name of Lillie Langtry. Her Bournemouth connection began shortly after Frank Miles, an artist, sketched her and her amazing beauty reached a very wide audience. Sir John Everett Millais' celebrated portrait gave her the name of the Jersey Lily. The Prince of Wales' (later Edward VII) interest was aroused. A meeting was arranged and Lillie became the first of his many mistresses to be accepted in public.

**142** Paul Verlaine enjoyed a more contented time in Bournemouth, as a tutor, from 1876-77, but on his return to Paris his life of debauchery continued.

**143** Lillie Langtry, the first official mistress of Edward VII, when Prince of Wales, pictured here after the painting by Millais; as a result, she was named 'the Jersey Lily'.

**144** *Langtry Manor Hotel*, built entirely to Lillie's choice and restored to its original likeness, with modern conveniences.

**145** The beautiful tiles of Shakespearean characters, all chosen by Lillie, were discovered hidden behind a blocked-up fireplace.

To meet in peace away from the ever-watchful eyes of enthusiastic Londoners, the prince arranged for a personal retreat to be built in the new watering place of Bournemouth. The large, red-bricked, red-tiled house, the upper part in Tudor style with black beams, was called the Red House and built entirely to Lillie's requirements. Just as her lover, she had a great disregard for conventions. On the minstrels' gallery was carved, 'THEY SAY, WHAT SAY THEY, LET THEM SAY'; on a beam in the palatial entrance hall is the hospitable greeting 'AND YOURS TOO MY FRIEND'. On the outside wall near Edward's bedroom were the words 'STET FORTUNA DOMUS'—'May fortune attend those who dwell here' and on an exterior wall near Lillie's suite 'DULCE DOMUM'—'a sweet home.'

The Red House has been a hotel for many years: firstly, *Manor Heath Hotel* and then the *Langtry Manor Hotel*. Rooms have been restored to their original state. Above a low, false ceiling in Edward's room an original oak-beamed one was revealed. An ornately carved wooden fireplace was discovered, and beautiful blue and gold tiles were revealed, depicting Shakespearean scenes, all of which had been chosen by Lillie.

Lillie lived in Bournemouth for about four years and entertained many people, including Oscar Wilde who performed at the Theatre Royal in 1883 and was a great admirer of hers. The story of Edward and Lillie has its place among the love stories of the past while the *Langtry Manor Hotel* survives as one of Bournemouth's listed buildings worthy of historic preservation.

**Guglielmo Marconi** was born in Bologna, Italy on 25 April 1874. He came to England after his experiments with electro-magnetism and a system of wireless communication had been rejected by the Ministry of Posts and Telegraphy in Rome.

Following successful demonstrations in London and on Salisbury Plain he established the world's first permanent wireless station at Alum Bay in the Isle of Wight in 1897 (it was dismantled June 1900). A second station was established in February 1898 at the *Madeira Hotel*, Bournemouth, now part of the Court Royal Miners' Convalescent Home. After a disagreement with the manager he moved his equipment to nearby Sandhills (now demolished). A 125-ft. mast was erected and experiments were carried out on small vessels near the Isle of Wight.

On 3 June 1898 Lord Kelvin, a famous scientist, had the privilege of sending the first paid radiogram, as he insisted on paying one shilling for each greeting sent to the receiving station in Bournemouth. In September Marconi moved to Sandbanks, Poole where he stayed at the *Haven Coaching Inn* (now the *Haven Hotel*). There he erected transmitting and receiving apparatus, a laboratory and workshop, including a 100-ft. mast. A plaque in the lounge proclaims his work and achievements there. His practical experiments led to the formation of the Marconi Wireless Telegraphy & Signal Co. Ltd. in 1897. For his successful work his name became celebrated throughout the world. He was awarded the K.C.V.O. by King George V, made a member of the Italian Senate and received the Albert Medal of the R.S.A.

**146**   The young Marconi with his apparatus for telegraphy without wires.

After several heart attacks he died in Rome on 20 July 1937, aged sixty-three. Through wireless communication news of his death was heard all over the world. News and music stations closed down for two minutes when the ether came as silent as in the days prior to Marconi's inventions.

**D.H. Lawrence**'s short association with Bournemouth was due to bad health, a breakdown, followed by tubercular pneumonia. On the advice of his doctor he came to Bournemouth on 6 January 1912 for a month's recuperation. To his friend, Edward Garnett, he wrote, 'I am actually going to Bournemouth on Saturday, to Compton House, St Peter's Rd.—a Boarding House. God help us'. On 7 January he wrote to Garnett:

> I don't like it very much. It's a sort of go-as-you-please boarding house where I shall be far more alone than if I had gone into apartments ... one is always churlish after illness. When I am better tempered I shall like the old maids and the Philistine men and the very proper proprietous maidens right enough. It is always raining—so stupid of it.[4]

To Jessie Chambers, his former sweetheart, he wrote,' I advise you never to come here for a holiday ... It's like a huge hospital. At every turn you come across invalids being pushed or pulled along. I shall be glad when I get away.' He managed to write a further 300 pages of the *Trespasser* which had been severely criticised.

**Gerald Durrell** was a conservationist and popular writer of amusing animal stories, Durrell was born in Jamshedpur, India, in 1925. The family spent some time in Bournemouth, but the cold, damp weather caused them to move to Corfu when Gerald was about eight years old. There he lived a carefree life among animals, insects and birds. When war seemed imminent the family were advised to return to England. After becoming assistant keeper at Whipsnade in 1945, Durrell

hoped to start his own zoo in Bournemouth. By then he had acquired many animals, all of which were kept in his sister Margo's garden in Bournemouth. Some even escaped, causing consternation in the neighbourhood. His attempts to start a zoo in Bournemouth and later in Poole lasted for a year and were met with 'stubborn refusal and myopic indifference'.[5] An introduction to Major Fraser of Les Augres Manor, Jersey, resulted, in three days, in the zoo that he had fought for 'for over a year with a fumbling bureaucracy in England'.[6] He died in March 1995.

Margo still lives in Bournemouth and writes amusing stories of the many adventures that happened to her and her family.

**Rupert Brooke** (1884-1915) stayed at Grantchester Dene in Dean Park Road (now holiday flats) when he was nine, to visit his grandfather and two aunts. During the First World War he was a frequent visitor as he was stationed at Blandford. He attended Holy Trinity Church several times, the last time shortly before Christmas 1914. To a friend he wrote, 'but now, alas! I shall expire vulgarly at Bournemouth and they will bury me on the shore near the bandstand' and 'I have been in this quiet place of invalids and gentlemanly sunsets for about 100 years, ever since yesterday week'. In 1915 he was sent out to the Mediterranean where he contracted a fatal illness. He was buried in Scyros on 23 April 1915.

**Charles Rolls**. In 1910, as part of Bournemouth's centenary celebrations, the first international aviation meeting was held. The joyous occasion was marred by the tragic death of the Hon. Charles Rolls, co-founder of Rolls-Royce, a motor car and balloon enthusiast and a skilled aviator. When the accident occurred he was flying a Short-Wright biplane and attempting to land on a marked spot. To the horror of spectators part of the tail-plane broke away when the machine hurtled down and, with a thud, turned over. He died shortly afterwards.

**147** Charles Stewart Rolls was killed in 1910 when flying a Short-Wright biplane at Bournemouth Centenary celebrations.

In 1978 a plaque was unveiled at the spot where he crashed at the end of the playing field of St Peter's School, which had been prepared as an aerodrome for the special display. His death is commemorated each year on 12 July with a cavalcade of early Rolls Royces.

**John Reuel Tolkien** (1892-1973), Professor of Anglo-Saxon and English Literature at Oxford University, achieved fame after the publication of *The Hobbit* and the *Lord of the Rings*.

His association with Bournemouth began through his wife, who enjoyed many happy holidays during the 1950s and 1960s at the *Miramar Hotel* on the East Cliff, where her health and spirits improved. When Tolkien retired they decided to live permanently in the area and bought a bungalow in Lakeside Road, Branksome Park. Although Tolkien missed the stimulating atmosphere of Oxford, they found new friends, particularly the local doctor and his wife, and they also became members of the Catholic church. They still paid frequent visits to the *Miramar* where they entertained their guests.

**148** John Reuel Tolkien, Professor of Anglo-Saxon and English, who with his wife enjoyed many happy hours at the *Miramar Hotel*, Bournemouth.

It was a shock to Tolkien when his wife died in 1971. After her death he returned to Oxford where he received many honours. He died in Bournemouth in September 1973 during a visit to his friends, Dr. and Mrs. Tolburst.

**Aubrey Beardsley** (1872-98) was a brilliant and erotic artist, who came to Bournemouth in 1896 suffering from tuberculosis. He stayed at first at *Pier View Hotel* (now demolished), Boscombe, an area which he disliked intensely.

After several haemorrhages, he moved, with his mother, to central Bournemouth and stayed at 'Muriel' (previously known as Cheam House) where he was converted to Catholicism at the Sacred Heart Church. His individualistic style of art nouveau often bordered on the fantastic. 'Muriel', described as a 'quirky' little building with semi-circular and octagonal bays, was demolished in 1996 for road widening,

when a beautifully carved mosaic based on an original Beardsley design, together with a plaque, was erected on the spot. He left Bournemouth in April 1897 for a warmer clime and died in Menton, France in March 1898.

## Other Famous People

So many well-known people have been associated with Bournemouth (and still are) that it is impossible to mention them all. Past residents include: **James Elroy Flecker**, who wrote the mournful poem 'Brumana' while on holiday as a schoolboy; **John Galsworthy** attended Saugeen Preparatory School for Boys in Derby Road. **Virginia Wade**, tennis player, lived in Bournemouth as a young girl when her father was vicar of Holy Trinity Church (now demolished). **Robin Cousins'** skating career owes much to visits to the Westover Road Ice Skating Rink (now closed).

149 *Miramar Hotel*, Bournemouth, where John Reuel Tolkien, enjoyed many happy holidays with his wife. They always had the same bedroom and even when they bought a house in the area they still entertained their guests at the *Miramar*.

John Creasey came to Bournemouth in 1939; he wrote about six hundred books (some under pseudonyms), mainly detective thrillers, some of which have been translated into 30 different languages. He lived at Alum Chine Avenue, then Nairn Road, followed by Wimborne Road and finally Bodenham, near Salisbury. A man of ideas, he stood as Liberal candidate and then started his own party, 'All Party Alliance'. **Beatrice Webb** (née Potter), born in 1858, came from a very wealthy family but was always concerned about poverty and the wretched conditions of work for many people. She went to a finishing school on Bath Hill (now a petrol station), attended Holy Trinity Church and had several holidays in Bournemouth. She married Sidney Webb, and both became prominent members of the Fabian Society. She spoke in Bournemouth on Poor Law Reform and similar subjects. **Roy Castle**, (1932-94) was born in Yorkshire, and bought a holiday home in Bournemouth in 1971 after a summer season there with Tom Jones at the Winter Gardens. There the family spent many happy times. He became even more famous after his performances with 'Record Breakers'. Both he and his wife Fiona faced bravely the traumatic period after Roy was diagnosed with cancer. **Tony Hancock** started his early career as a comedian in Bournemouth, where his parents, who had been music-hall entertainers, owned the *Durley Court Hotel* in Gervis Road. He owed his start to George Fairweather, a local Bournemouth entertainer. Tony Hancock brought laughter into the lives of many with his genius for provocative and brash remarks, but behind the humour was a worried man, unsure of his skill, who found refuge in drink, with unfortunate results. Others were **Sydney Horler, PC Wren, Bill Cotton, Anita Harris, Tony Blackburn, Mantovani, Freddie Mills** and **Ken Baily**, usually seen in grey suit and topper decorated with the colours of the Union Jack at most civic and social events in Bournemouth. He died on 16 December 1993 aged 82 years.

**150** Beatrice Webb, a great philanthropist, worked to improve the conditions of the poor. She stayed in Bournemouth on several occasions. (The photograph was taken by George Bernard Shaw.)

## Bournemouth's Russian Colony

Few traces remain today of Bournemouth's Russian connection at the turn of the century. From 1897 a number of Russian exiles, who had fled from Czarist oppression, formed a settlement in the little village of Tuckton. Alexander II was known as the liberator of the downtrodden serfs, but when he was assassinated in March 1881, Alexander III, a despotic ruler who succeeded him, shelved most of his reforms.

The colony was headed by Count Vladimir Tchertkoff, formerly a great favourite at the Imperial Russian Court. When he decided to quit his life of dissipation at the court and to

**151** Count Tchertkoff working with Tolstoy in Russia.

**152** Countess Tchertkoff had a holiday home, *Slavanka*, in Southbourne.

devote his time to helping poor serfs, he was given the choice of exile or police supervision in a small Baltic town. Together with about thirty other intellectuals, he decided to come to England. The group bought an old house with 20 bedrooms at 61 Saxonbury Road, Tuckton, and an old water-works in Iford Lane, Tuckton, which had been erected in 1875 by the Bournemouth Gas & Water Co. to pump water from the river Stour to the Southbourne water tower. The venture proved unsuccessful, owing to quantities of silt and sand in the water, and by 1898 the pumping station was sold. The building remained empty until it was purchased by Tchertkoff, who realised its possibility as a printing works where the banned writings of Count Leo Tolstoy could be published.

It is often wondered why the unknown hamlet of Tuckton, then surrounded by woods, cornfields and a few cottages, was chosen by the colony. Count Tchertkoff's mother had a holiday residence in nearby Southbourne, called *Slavanka* (Place of Glory) where she passed many happy holidays. Tchertkoff hoped that the health-giving properties of the Southbourne spa would improve the health of his wife.

Madame Tchertkoff was said to be one of the most interesting Christian women in the world. As a young countess she often came to Britain and knew Queen Victoria very well and her family.

At Tuckton House the colony lived simply. They practiced a Christian type of communism by sharing all their possessions. There was little personal comfort in the house; everything was utilitarian and spotlessly clean, and there were army beds in the sleeping quarters. They were vegetarians and grew their own food. Visitors were always welcome to partake of their simple meals. Russian type-face was shipped to the printing works so that the works of Tolstoy could be printed. Tolstoy made Tchertkoff his literary agent outside Russia. At the printing works the Free Age Press was established, and books were sold cheaply with no copyright. Refugees were employed as compositors, printers and binders. Everywhere the Slav tongue could be heard. Here many of Tolstoy's philosophical and religious pamphlets and works were produced and shipped through private channels back to Russia, and to other countries where Russians were living.

The refugees also produced a 16-page prohibited newspaper. In order to smuggle copies into Russia a special edition was printed on thin rice paper and slipped into an envelope as an ordinary letter. Many of Tolstoy's works, some of which were translated into different languages, gave information about the suffering of those who were oppressed.

**153** Tuckton House, Saxonbury Road, where the Russian refugees lived from 1898-1908. They lived simply and were well-liked.

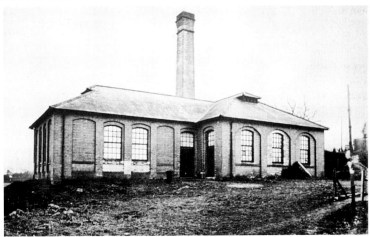

**154** The old printing works at Iford Lane, Tuckton, where many of Tolstoy's works were printed.

Originally the manuscripts received from Tolstoy were kept in strong boxes at Tuckton House. In 1906, to safeguard them further a specially constructed strongroom was built with reinforced 18-in.-thick concrete walls and steel grill doors. There were no windows and the roof was fireproof and even earthquake proof; alarm bells were switched on every night.

In 1908 Tchertkoff was overjoyed to be given permission to return to Russia to live near Tolstoy, to assist him and to continue working for the peasants' welfare.

Wealthy Countess Tchertkoff donated vast sums of money towards the improvement of the slums in St Petersburg. For this she fell out of favour with the authorities and only just managed to escape, although her husband was executed by the Czarist regime. In 1917, exiled and penniless, she returned to *Slavanka* in Southbourne, accompanied by Anna Pinikoski, an old family nurse. Slavanka was sold to a syndicate of businessmen and in 1921 became a Christian conference centre. Countess Tchertkoff was able to remain there for the rest of her life. She died in 1922 and was buried in Christchurch cemetery where her gravestone was inscribed 'Madame Elizabeth Tchertkoff, one of the first of Russian nobility to accept Christ, through the ministry of Lord Radstock, who fell asleep in Christ, 25 January 1922, aged 91.'

Among the exiles was an Estonian, Ludwig Perno, who returned to Russia in 1917 after the Russian Revolution. Because of his pacifist views, he was forced to flee with his wife, who had been imprisoned in Siberia for bringing educational ideas to the people. Together with their baby daughter they escaped to England and in 1922 they again stayed at Tuckton House. In 1929, however, Tuckton House was sold to Mrs. C. Angus as a nursing home. Perno was given power of attorney for documents still remaining in this country. He continued to live in the Southbourne area where he translated many of Tolstoy's pamphlets into English and other languages.

On the retirement of Mrs. Angus in 1965 Tuckton House was sold to property developers and was demolished to be replaced by an estate of bungalows. The demolition of the Russians' strongroom proved exceedingly difficult. After working for a week, labourers had only managed to cut a hole 15ins. in diameter because of the thickness of the walls. Many people have bitterly regretted the destruction of the unique building where the works of Tolstoy had been so securely stored. The printing works was bought by Harry W. Kiddle & Sons in 1918, and where the first motor-car body and motor-coach body in Bournemouth were built.

In 1988 the old print works and area were acquired by a development firm who renovated the works and built several houses which incorporate the original arched façades at the front and the 'listed' chimney behind the houses.

It is good to know that, under our democratic system, persecuted Russians were able to come here and to publish some of the forbidden works of Tolstoy.

**Rev. and Frances Yorke-Batley** In 1924 Rev. and Mrs. Yorke-Batley purchased a boys' preparatory school, the Wychwood School in Bournemouth, in partnership with J.B. Calkin, an eminent archaeologist who had made many exciting discoveries on Henistbury Head, the mound of antiquity of which Bournemouth is justly proud. Many famous boys attended the school, including members of the Beale family, Group Captain Peter Townsend and Gerald Durrell. In 1938 the school was sold again and, in the 1970s, the school, with its attractive towers and turrets, was demolished for redevelopment.

After resuming parish work in Corfe Castle, Rev. Yorke-Batley retired in 1948 and returned to Bournemouth. Shortly afterwards, to his surprise, he was invited to become the Actors' Church Union Chaplain at the Pavilion Theatre. After some hesitation he and his wife decided to invite the artistes to tea at their house in Boscombe whereupon, in a friendly atmosphere, they would be able to help those who had many problems. The parties were a great success. Rev. Yorke-Batley died in 1960 and his widow felt unable to continue without his support, but was persuaded by Leslie Crowther, one of the earliest visitors, to continue the parties which meant so much to the travelling artistes.

The parties were eventually discontinued in 1989. Throughout their 25-year existence, albums of photographs had been collected; they read like a Who's Who, chronicling early lives of then unknown stars to their fame of today.

Mrs. Yorke-Batley and her friend and companion, Miss Meade, were awarded Hearts of Gold on Esther Rantzen's television programme, when they were greeted by Leslie Crowther, Hinge and Bracket, Little and Large, Ruth Madoc and many other 'party visitors'. Shortly afterwards Mrs. Yorke-Batley received a British Empire medal in the Queen's New Year Honours List, in recognition of her services to the theatre and artistes in Bournemouth. Mrs. Yates-Batley died in 1996, and a commemoration plaque was erected in the Pavilion Theatre in Bournemouth, in a ceremony attended by actors, family and friends from all over the country.

## They Came and Stayed

**Max Bygraves** came to Bournemouth in *c.*1969 when he was rich, popular and very famous. Surprisingly, his first major summer show in Bournemouth was not until 1996, whilst producers from all over the world clamour for his performances. At 75 years young, he is active, enjoys each day, his successful career, his happy marriage to Blossom, his growing family and beautiful home in Bournemouth.

**Edna Dawes**, a prolific international author, whose 30 novels and sagas have been translated into many languages, came to Bournemouth in 1978. Many of her books have been written under pseudonyms, her lucky E.D.s, as she calls them. At present she writes military history

**155** Max Bygraves the entertainer, still making people laugh.

**156** Edna Dawes, the internationally famous author who has written over 30 books and sagas that have been translated into many languages.

**157** Jack Inglis the model maker, seen here working on a scale model of Big Ben for the British Travel Authority.

**158** Vernon Preston, international lookalike of H.R.H. Prince Philip, Duke of Edinburgh.

under the name of **Edna Drummond** and military aviation under the name of **Elizabeth Darrell**, while finding inspiration from her many journeys abroad and the delights of the beautiful Dorset country.

**Jack Inglis** was born in St Andrew's, Fife in 1931. An actor, producer, stage designer and model-maker, he left fame and the busy life of London because of ill-health. With his partner, Bill Maguire, a clever stage technician, he came to Bournemouth to enjoy life among the pines and beaches in a more restful existence. They are still involved in model making and marionettes and are lecturers for U.3.A., Jack on 'Musical Appreciation' and Bill on 'Painting for Pleasure'.

**Vernon Preston** has lived in Bournemouth for over 12 years, loving the sea in its varying moods, the sand and tree-lined chines. The many remarks made on his likeness to Prince Philip caused him to become a popular lookalike, but wherever he travels as a 'royal' celebrity, he always enjoys returning to beautiful Bournemouth.

**Irene Richmond**, actress, said 'good-bye' to London and its many theatres after visiting Bournemouth on holiday and decided to make this lovely seaside resort her home. She has now become a well-known speaker on her fascinating, and often amusing, life on the stage. She was a tutor for the University of the Third Age (U.3.A.) on Poetry for Pleasure and now leads a poetry group at the New Church, Tuckton.

**Desmond Tarrant**, a well-known poet and writer of intellectual novels, has lived in the Bournemouth area since 1939. He has taught English and American literature at the Universities of London, Strathclyde, Southampton and in America. He thinks Lillie Langtry and Edward VII must have walked through his grounds in Cassel Avenue, which used to be dense woodland, on their way to visit their friend, Sir Ernest Cassel, grandfather of Edwina Ashley Mountbatten, who was a former owner of Branksome Dene.

**Bournemouth Natural Science Society** has its origins in the Bournemouth Natural History Society from 1868-82 and then Bournemouth Scientific & Antiquarian Society from 1883-97. From 1903-10 it was known as the Bournemouth & District Society of Natural Science. It adopted its present name in 1910 and purchased its own premises in 1920, a Grade II Listed Victorian, four-storey villa at 39 Christchurch Road, Bournemouth.

The house was built in 1877/8 on land bought from the Meyrick Estate and was sold to Henry Joy, a well-known builder and carpenter, for £800. Joy had already built Southbourne Terrace, the first six high-class shops on the north side of the Square, Gervis Arcade and, later, Westbourne Arcade.

The house was originally called Bassendean and was sold on a 93-year lease. It included a double drawing-room, dining-room, library, 10 bedrooms and many other rooms. It had 17 chimneys. The building changed hands many times before the end of the First World War. The Society had used rooms at the Municipal College at the Lansdowne for several years until they were required for extra educational classes. Fortunately the Society was able to acquire the lease and then the freehold for £800 from the Meyrick Estate. Soon an extension in the form of a large lecture theatre, to seat 200 people, was erected in the spacious grounds.

During the last war the Society's activities continued, although part of the building was used as an air raid warden's post, and the library was occupied by the Central Office Supply Services. In 1959 some of the still extensive grounds were sold for £9,000, enabling the Society to carry out much needed repairs, including a new concrete floor and heating system.

Among its Egyptian antiquities is a reconstruction showing what the head of an Egyptian mummy would have looked like when alive. There are also displays of birds, insects, butterflies through the ages, while lectures are given on Astronomy, History, Botany, Geology and many other subjects.

**159** Irene Richmond, actress, now a well-known speaker on her acting career.

**160** Desmond Tarrant M.A., poet and author.

## CHAPTER ELEVEN

# Endpiece

The development of Bournemouth in 190 years from uncultivated wasteland to a fashionable coastal resort is considered unique. Its former image of bathchairs, invalids and an élite class has been replaced by a popular holiday area and a town with almost 170,000 people. Bournemouth, with its seven miles of golden sands and gorse-clad cliffs, now attracts a wide range of visitors from around the world.

The Victorian character of the town diminishes yearly due to demolition in the interests of so-called progress: the need for more modern roads, high-rise flats and office buildings. Fortunately many buildings of historic interest are retained as a reminder of the town's early heritage.

Several fine Victorian churches are still to be seen, designed by eminent architects such as G.E. Street, Decimus Burton, Norman Shaw and J.D. Sedding.

The Gothic form was considered most appropriate for religious buildings, Roman for secular buildings while Victorian villas range from Italianate to Tudor. Ornamental details—differently-shaped gables, curved arches, gazebos and cast-iron balconies are reminders of a bygone age when a queen was on the throne for more than sixty years. A much admired modern church is the elegant Punshon Church in Exeter Road, designed by Ronald Sims (see Chapter Three).

Bournemouth, like most pleasant coastal resorts, attracts a high percentage of retired residents, but the needs of the young are also cared for. Many educational and cultural facilities attract students from home and overseas. Bournemouth & Poole College of Further Education specialises in business and commerce, while Bournemouth University now has over 19,000 students and offers a wide variety of courses and degrees, including media studies, television, computer technology, and is considered one of the top hotel and restaurant training centres.

The Bournemouth Centre of Community Arts is housed in one of the first Free Church schools in Boscombe, *c.*1875. Today it provides practical and creative courses for many Dorset schoolchildren, including art, drama and other exciting projects. Mentally handicapped come along and find inspiration from its variety of active and expressionistic groups. Adults come there, too, for concerts and plays. Members of the University of the Third Age (U.3.A.) used to have their offices in the building and attended classes there. U.3.A. is now housed in the Pokedown Centre, 896 Christchurch Road, where most of the classes are held. The building is the headquarters of Help & Care who provide a wide range of services to assist older people to live in greater comfort and security in their own homes. Interesting historic walks are organised each year by the Office of Tourism. Yes, there is plenty to do in Bournemouth.

Hotels and holiday flats abound. The *Royal Bath Hotel*, the first purpose-built hotel in Bournemouth, has maintained its five-star status for many years. The *Carlton*, which started as a 'Boarding Establishment for Gentlefolk' after a group of businessmen purchased a fine, Victorian villa, 'Brumstath', is now owned by Derbyshire Menzies Hotel Group and was awarded four stars by the A.A. after a spectacular refurbishment.

In the main, industry and residential areas have been kept apart. Recently, however, some of Bournemouth's tranquillity seems to have disappeared through increased traffic congestion, the growth of discos, casinos and nightclubs and a greater number of public houses.

Thomas Hardy's description of 'Sandbourne' (Bournemouth) as a city of detached and fanciful residences applies less. His remark that it is a Mediterranean lounging place on the English Channel still seems appropriate, as perhaps do the words of Betjeman, 'Bournemouth is a stately Victorian duchess with her head touching Christchurch and her feet turned towards Poole'. *Pulchritudo et Salubritas*—beauty and health: long may this apply to our town of Bournemouth.

**161**   The beach and cliffs at Bournemouth, *c*.1947—and no high-rise flats.

# NOTES

## Chapter Four

1. Mate, Charles H. and Riddle, Charles, *Bournemouth 1810-1910: The History of a Modern Health and Pleasure Resort* (1910)

## Chapter Six

1. State Papers Domestic, Elizabeth I, vol. 97, no. 32
2. In Red House Museum
3. Young, David S., *The Story of Bournemouth* (1957)
4. Lands, S.J., *The Growth of Winton* (1976)
5. Dyson, Taylor, *The History of Christchurch* (1954)

## Chapter Ten

1. Award Map 1805, Lansdowne Reference Library, Bournemouth
2. Ordnance Map 1811, Red House Museum
3. Ordnance Map 1870, Red House Museum
4. Huxley, Aldous, *Letters of D.H. Lawrence* (1932)
5. Durrell, Gerald, *The Stationary Ark* (1976)
6. *ibid.*

# Bibliography

Ashley, Harry and Hugh, *Bournemouth, 1890-1990*

Bishop, Barbara, *Secondary Education in Bournemouth from 1902 to present day* (1966)

Boulton, James T., *Lawrence in Love, D.H. Lawrence to Louie Burrows* (1968)

Brough, James, *The Prince and the Lily* (1975)

Bruce, George, *A Fortune and a Family—Bournemouth and the Cooper-Deans* (1987)

Busby, Frederick, *The Story of Holy Trinity, Bournemouth. 1867-1953* (1953)

Castle, Roy, *Now and Then—An Autobiography* (1996)

Chacksfield, K. Merle, *Smuggling Days* (1966)

Chilver, Kathleen M., *Holdenhurst, Mother of Bournemouth* (1956)

Compton, Thomas A., *Southbourne's Infancy* (1914)

Cook, K.M., *St Mary's Gate, 1886-1986*

Dale, Richard, *Reminiscences of Stourfield, by Mr Dale of Tuckton* (1876)

Darwin, Francis, *The Life and Letters of Darwin* (3 vols., 1887)

Davies, John T., *Richmond Hill Story* (1956)

Dobel, Horace, *On the Mont Dore Cure* (1881)

Durrell, Gerald, *My Family and Other Animals* (1956)

Durrell, Margo, *Whatever Happened to Margo?* (1996)

Edwards, Elizabeth, *A History of Bournemouth* (1981)

Ford, R., *The History of Bournemouth Police* (1963)

Forse, Rev. E.J.G., *Fifty Years of Southbourne Parish, 1876-1926* (1926)

Godfrey, Sir Dan, *Memories and Music, 35 Years of Conducting* (1924)

Graham, Mary, *The Royal National Hospital—The Story of Bournemouth's Sanatorium* (1992)

Hammerton, J.A., *Stevensoniana, An Anecodotal Life and Appreciation of Robert Louis Stevenson* (1907)

Hughes, Ted, *Bournemouth Fireman at War* (1991)

Jolly, W.P., *Marconi* (1972)

Jones, John Daniel, *Three Score Years and Ten, the Autobiography of J.D. Jones* (1940)

McQueen, Ian, *Bournemouth St Peter's* (1971)

Mate, Charles H. and Riddle, Charles, *Bournemouth 1810-1910: The History of a Modern Health & Pleasure Resort* (1910)

Miller, Geoffrey, *The Bournemouth Symphony Orchestra* (1970)

Lord Montagu of Beaulieu, *Rolls of Rolls Royce, A Biography* (1966)

Olding, Simon and Garner, Shaun, *So Fair a House—The Story of Russell-Cotes Art Gallery & Museum* (1997)

Russell-Cotes, Sir Merton, *Home and Abroad* (2 vols., 1921)

Street, Sean and Carpenter, Ray, *Bournemouth Symphony Orchestra, A Centenary Celebration, 1893-1993* (1993)

Taconis, Mrs. F.M., *Russian Colony at Tuckton, 1897-1908* (1918)

Talbot, Mary Anne, *The History of Talbot Village* (1873)

Young, David, *The Story of Bournemouth* (1957)

# Index